ON THE HILL

ON THE HILL

A Photographic History of the University of Kansas

Second Edition, Revised

Compiled by

Virginia Adams
Katie Armitage
Donna Butler
Carol Shankel
Barbara Watkins

with a foreword by Raymond Nichols
and introductory essays by Roy E. Gridley

University Press of Kansas

As we compiled *On the Hill,* many people shared photographs or information concerning the University or gave us support in various ways. The contributions of John Nugent, Ned Kehde, Barry Bunch, and Thomas Ryther of the University Archives have been indispensable. Others who helped locate photos for the second edition, which updates the book from 1980 to 1992, are Doug Koch at University Relations, Mary Ann Saunders of KU Endowment, Justin Knutt at the UDK, and Crissy Causey at the Sports Information office. For their advice and encouragement we also want to thank Thomas Averill, Steven Jansen, B. J. Pattee, James Scally, Steven Skaggs, Thomas Southall, Jane Stevens, Allen Wiechert, and Richard Wintermote. Jonathan Blumb restored a number of the photographs included here, and Janet Moore designed chapter 8.

Many people who were part of the University's history do not appear in these pages because of limitations of space or unavailability of photographs. We hope that the spirit, if not the image, of these individuals is represented here.

Publication of the first edition made possible by the Kansas University Endowment Association.

The paper used in this publication meets the minimum requirements of the American National Standard for Permanence of Paper for Printed Library Materials Z39.48-1984.

Published by the University Press of Kansas (Lawrence, Kansas 66049), which was organized by the Kansas Board of Regents and is operated and funded by Emporia State University, Fort Hays State University, Kansas State University, Pittsburg State University, the University of Kansas, and Wichita State University

Library of Congress Cataloging-in-Publication Data

On the hill : a photographic history of the University of Kansas / compiled by Virginia Adams . . . [et al.] ; with a foreword by Raymond Nichols and introductory essays by Roy E. Gridley.—2nd ed., rev.
    p.   cm.
Includes index.
ISBN 0-7006-0611-4
1. University of Kansas—History. 2. University of Kansas—Pictorial works. I. Adams, Virginia, 1921–   .
LD2688.05   1993
378.781'65—dc20   93-1258

Printed in the United States of America

10 9 8 7 6 5 4 3 2 1

Contents

Foreword

I came to Lawrence in the fall of 1922 as a naïve, unsophisticated freshman from a central-western Kansas high school. The Santa Fe train snaked along the Kaw River to the station and delivered me on the platform with my sense of direction ninety degrees off compass. Despite this handicap and the fact that this was my first visit to Lawrence and the University, I readily adjusted to the new environment and soon developed an appreciation of the University that was to grow into an affection shared by many KU graduates. My association with the University has continued through five chancellorships and my own service as chancellor.

From my perspective, a major characteristic of the University has been change—in the physical size of the campus, in the addition and replacement of buildings, in composition of the faculty and administration, in the curricula. One of the few constant features on Mount Oread has been the power plant whistle that announces the start and end of classes. Even the familiar skyline has changed. The smokestack and the tower of Dyche Museum remain, but the red towers of old Fraser Hall are gone. The Campanile is now the commanding feature of the skyline.

But more significant than change is the thread of consistency that has dominated the KU story—the people's continued belief in and support of higher education, the continued dedication to the lofty goals of a quality university as visualized by the early faculty, and the continued magnanimity of alumni and friends, whose gifts support programs of a quality that state appropriations alone do not provide.

Over the years my classmates have observed this ever-changing university on pilgrimages to the campus. Those who date back to the decades before 1950 find that the relaxed, provincial university of their day has been transformed into a fast-moving international university, with students from many countries studying subjects unheard of in the past— computer science, space technology, nuclear power, genetic engineering.

Many buildings of my student generation are gone, replaced by modern structures that retain their old names: Fraser Hall, which stresses utility rather than architectural beauty; Blake Hall, which accommodates political science rather than physics; Robinson Gymnasium and Haworth Hall, which were rebuilt in new locations in order to make way for the new humanities building, Wescoe Hall. Buildings new to my generation include Summerfield Hall for economics and business; Murphy Hall for theater, music, and speech; Malott Hall for chemistry, physics, and pharmacy; Learned Hall for the engineering sciences, which released Marvin Hall for the expanding program in architecture; the Art and Design Building, which combines in one location the once far-scattered work in art; new Green Hall, Allen Field House, and Nichols Hall, the interdisciplinary space science center on West Campus.

Several generations of students following World War II will remember the temporary buildings hastily moved onto campus from closed military bases to hold classes for the "G.I. bulge" of students released from military service. With three exceptions, these buildings have been razed.

Perhaps the most striking change is the development of a student housing system. In my day, Corbin Hall was the only dormitory. Today, the dormitory system provides housing for five thousand students. Most of these structures, including three hundred apartments for married graduate students, are located on picturesque Daisy Hill. Few of the three-story rooming houses that accommodated so many generations of students remain in operation.

An important change is the expansion of the campus onto land acquired by the Endowment Association. This expansion includes the 480 acres of land west of Iowa Street added to protect future growth of the campus and the acreage southwest of the original campus now occupied by Summerfield Hall, Murphy Hall, new Green Hall, the Field House, and the dormitories on Daisy Hill.

The composition of the faculty naturally has changed. Gone are favorite professors. Familiar names have disappeared as retirement, death, or moves to other institutions have taken their toll. I recall with special appreciation my rhetoric teacher, Helen Rhoda Hoopes, for her insistence on strict attention to grammar and the development of clear, concise prose; my professor in American literature, Edwin M. Hopkins, whose technique of answering a question with a question taught me to search on my own for the answer; and F. H. Hodder, whose two-semester course in presidential administration using original library resources as a textbook taught me the basic methods of careful library research. Other students have their own lists of favorite professors, some of whom no doubt were Eugenie Galloo and Elise Neuen-Schwander in French; R. C. Moore in geology; Cora Downs in bacteriology; H. P. Cady, R.

Q. Brewster, and A. W. Davidson in chemistry; U. G. Mitchell and Florence Black in mathematics; and Ralph Major, H. C. Tracy, H. R. Wahl, T. G. Orr, and F. C. Neff in medicine. My classmates and I are gratified to know that successors to the notable faculty of yesteryear today maintain the classroom teaching excellence and the scholarly productivity of their predecessors.

Each student generation fondly recalls the events and experiences of its own university years. My university years were unfairly characterized as the "Age of Flaming Youth" by *College Humor* magazine, by the cartoons of John Held, Jr., in the old *Life* magazine, and by F. Scott Fitzgerald's *This Side of Paradise.* Such exaggerations, my classmates and I believe, did not apply to our university. It is true that our generation had fun, but we also prized solid academic achievement.

Many of our memorable traditions have disappeared. We participated in the Nightshirt Parade, an event held the night before the first home football game. The men students assembled on campus dressed in nightshirts or pajamas, marched to Massachusetts Street, then snake-danced down the street to a bonfire and a rally at the bridge, followed by free movies. Most freshmen enjoyed the required wearing of the freshman "beanie," even under enforcement by K-men. We also enjoyed the Doc Yak show, a football rally conducted from the bed of a hayrack parked near Green Hall. "Pep pills" (red hots) were dispensed to the students in attendance.

Some of us participated in campus politics, either in the Black Mask or the Pachacamac party, and marched in the pre-election torchlight parades. We no longer swim in Potter Lake; or publish the *Sour Owl,* a so-called humor magazine whose contents consisted principally of reprints of suggestive jokes from magazines of other campuses, or the *Dove,* a journal of student opinion on campus, state and national issues, printed on pink paper to suggest a liberal point of view.

Even in the 1920s some traditions were on their way out. Gone are the baseball game between faculty and seniors at the end of spring semester (so few students attended the game in my senior year that in order to field a team the captain had to recruit players from the spectators, including me) and the annual competition of freshmen and upperclassmen to determine whether freshmen should continue to wear their beanies. Freshmen usually won the tug of war across Potter Lake.

Gone also are all-night farewell parties at the end of the spring semester; favorite rendezvous points such as Brick's Cafe, Wiedemann's Tea Room, the Blue Mill, and the Dine-a-Mite Cafe; mid-morning convocations with speakers of distinction but indifferent student attendance; the Community Lecture Course, an evening event that brought distinguished lecturers to the campus; the foreign film series on Friday evenings in Hoch Auditorium; Van the Animal Man, caretaker of laboratory animals whom students remember as the man who led a sheep across the campus; Mary Neustifter, switch-board operator who personalized telephone service; and George Snyder, the sole traffic officer who took in good grace the tricks played on him by students.

The activity that most characterized the 1920s was dancing. There were Wednesday afternoon tea dances, weekend Varsity dances and the Freshman Frolic, Soph Hop, Junior Prom, Senior Cake Walk, Law Scrim, and Hobnail Hop. It was the era of ballroom dancing, program dances, and big name bands such as the Paul Whiteman Band.

The 1920s were notable for the establishment by the 1925 legislature of the bipartisan Board of Regents for supervision of state-supported colleges and universities. This action was prompted by the firing of Chancellor Lindley by the Board of Administration, the agency then in charge of higher education, for his refusal to make faculty and staff appointments dictated by the governor.

I remember the 1930s as lean years in terms of legislative support and opportunities for jobs. Major events of the decade were the dust storms and the Great Depression. The federally funded National Youth Administration student

job program made university attendance possible for several hundred students. To feed these students, cafeteria director Hermina Zipple initiated the ten-cent meal plan. At the end of the decade the University faced the charge of on-campus communist influence by the family of former student Don Henry, who died while serving in the ambulance corps in the Spanish Civil War.

In the 1940s the major event was the disruption of university classwork by calls to military service in World War II, leaving behind a largely female enrollment. What followed was the transformation of quiet Mount Oread into a busy military training base including the machinist mate program for the Navy, the Army Specialized Training Program, the V-12 program for the Navy, and medicine for both Army and Navy. Malott Hall, Fowler Shops, more than half of Strong Hall, and several fraternity houses were diverted to military uses.

I recall the 1950s as an era of overcrowded classrooms and housing. Fourteen hundred students were accommodated in facilities at the Sunflower Ordnance Works near DeSoto. Young people, released from military service at the end of the war, flocked to the University to start or renew their studies under the "GI Bill of Rights." In this decade KU basketball enjoyed a golden era, three times playing in the NCAA finals. The Campanile was erected in memory of those who gave their lives in World War II.

The troubled days of the 1960s are remembered principally for student dissent and activism over social conditions such as segregation or equal rights, and by protest against militarism, especially the involvement in Vietnam, or against "irrelevant" courses. The public demanded strong action against such acts as disruption of the annual R.O.T.C. review, parades in opposition to the Vietnam War, and takeover of offices in support of demands for minority representation in activities and the governance system. At issue was the right of free speech—the right to militantly support a cause. That the University survived this period without major tragedies was a victory of administrative willingness to bend but not to break. It is notable that despite disruption and misdirection, six students in seven years won coveted Rhodes scholarships.

Although the early 1970s was punctuated by the burning of the Kansas Union and the bombing of the computer center, the period is remembered for its gradual transition from activism to willingness to work through normal channels to accomplish change. For me, the major event of the decade came in August of 1972 when the Board of Regents asked me to serve as chancellor for the school year, succeeding Chancellor Chalmers, who had resigned. I accepted the challenge with reservations about my ability to bring to an end the period of disruption. Fortunately, the faculty, the student body, and the public responded to my efforts. This unity of purpose resulted in the effective transition to more normal operations. My successor, Archie Dykes, continued to reestablish the confidence of the Kansas public in the University.

For more than half a century, alumni and friends of the University have regularly demonstrated their concern for the institution through their gifts to the University through the Endowment Association. Student financial need has been met by such generous gifts as the Summerfield scholarships. Housing needs have been eased by the gifts of Mrs. Elizabeth Watkins and Mr. and Mrs. Joseph R. Pearson. Quality of instruction has been advanced by buildings and equipment gifts by Oscar Stauffer and Mr. and Mrs. Ralph "Bud" Weir. The cultural environment has been enriched by the magnificent benefactions of Kenneth and Helen Spencer. Thousands of gifts each year, in the main unrestricted as to usage, have augmented the institutional resources in faculty research, awards for teaching excellence, and library acquisitions. Alumni generosity has indeed made possible a University of higher quality than state support alone can provide.

Each year thousands of alumni and former students return to the campus to attend athletic events, drawn by recollections of performances in earlier years by such participants as Glenn Cunningham, Al Oerter, Jim Ryun, Jim Bausch, Ray Evans, Gale Sayers, Wilt Chamberlain, and Clyde Lovellette. They attend anniversary occasions, such as the celebration of their graduation, hold reunions of their social groups, or visit their own children now at the University. Still others return to serve on advisory committees to their professional schools or the Alumni or Endowment Associations. Such response to the calls of Alma Mater are most important to institutional efforts to establish quality programs.

Since the University opened its doors in the fall of 1866, the primary concern of its leaders has been the level of legislative support. Private giving has allowed the University to supplement state support to draw closer to realizing our dream of excellence. That the University is close to the realization of that dream is indicated by the high rating given in the 1981 publication by the *New York Times* of *A Selective Guide to College Admission.* KU ranked among the leading state-supported universities of the United States.

And today as we stand on Mount Oread to gaze across the "enchanted valleys of the Wakarusa and the Kaw," to employ a phrase used by John J. Ingalls at the first commencement in 1873, we do so with love for our University and pride in its accomplishments.

Raymond Nichols
Chancellor Emeritus
1983

ON THE HILL

Mount Oread, 1867

Mr. Gardner, a photographic artist from Washington City, is in Lawrence having come to Kansas for the purpose of taking photographic views of remarkable and noted places in our state.

Kansas Daily Tribune, September 21, 1867

The University of Kansas had been open for one year when Alexander Gardner photographed Mount Oread.

CHAPTER ONE

The Early Years

THE UNIVERSITY OF KANSAS evolved from an aspiration common to many communities being founded in the new western states just before and after the Civil War: the desire to crown their fair city with an academy, a college, or even a "state university," whatever that might mean. Many such colleges were founded and housed in rather imposing single buildings; most failed and became "ghost colleges" of the kind that dot the map of Kansas. Territorial Kansas was deeply and violently divided between free- and slave-state supporters, who themselves were split into factions. Each of the constitutions proposed by the contending parties called for the creation of a state university. The question was not if Kansas would have such an institution, but which town would receive "the greatest boon that can be conferred upon any community," in the words of the *Lawrence Herald of Freedom* in 1856. Soon after statehood came in 1861 and the passage of the Morrill land-grant college act of 1862, the legislature chose to transform the Methodist Bluemont Central College at Manhattan into Kansas' land-grant college. Had Kansas followed the pattern of adjacent states like Nebraska or Missouri or more settled states like Wisconsin or Illinois, the state university and the land-grant college of Kansas would have been a single, unified institution. But some Kansans—particularly those with a stake in an ambitious town—believed the constitution called for a state "university" in addition to a

land-grant "college." Lawrence citizens had by 1859 quite literally laid the foundation for such an institution, as the lithograph on page 14 shows. Altruistic belief in higher education and civic improvement mixed with individual self-interest, political manipulation, and legislative chicanery to finally bring state authorization for a building to be completed on that foundation which had lain abandoned throughout the Civil War. In the autumn a year after war's end, the "University of Kansas" was opened in the building to become known as Old North College.

For the early years of the University, the photographic record is a scanty one. Of the few photos taken, fewer have survived. Those that did are, in their content, rather spare. The outline of the Hill against the sky, two buildings by the early seventies, all in formal black and white, evoke a stern, even stark, simplicity. On the eve of the Civil War, an artist set up his easel near the site of the first University building. Looking northeast, he recorded the Kaw Valley and the town beginning to move out from its clustered center. He gives nearly half of his space to the sky, beneath which a workman shapes stone, wagons and buggies roll along the roads, parasoled women stroll: the artist has created a sense of life and motion the camera will be unable to catch for decades to come. Two years after the war ended, Alexander Gardner set up his camera near a corral to the west of the old Hogback Ridge, or

The early attempt to build a college on the hill (artist unknown), 1859

Devil's Backbone, now on its way to becoming Mount Oread. North College has a tenuous foothold on the far northern brow. Five years later, "the largest and doubtless the best planned college edifice in the United States," University Hall, anchors the southern rim; there, the grounds were graded and sown and protected from wandering cows by hedge, stone fence, and iron gate. What the camera has turned to shades of gray were really "broad expanses of living green," Walt Whitman tells us. That was early summer. In the autumn of 1866, when Lillian Robinson struggled up the hill from the east to "read in Greek, recite in Latin," the knee-high grass would have turned reddish-yellow, the few clumps of sumac turned scarlet. The sky was, without doubt, blue. The place appears as simple and straightforward as the prose of the newspaper advertisement that announced the opening of the University of Kansas on Wednesday, September 12, 1866, with the $30 tuition "payable in advance."

During the early years, then, only the essentials. The early benefactor, Amos Lawrence, a Massachusetts manufacturer who had already helped establish Lawrence University in Wisconsin, gave $10,000 to found what he hoped would be called "Free State College" in memory of those who had died in the antislavery struggle. The Reverend R. W. Oliver, who acted without pay as first chancellor, unsuccessfully sought from the Regents some definition of his duties. In 1868 he was succeeded by John Fraser, a man with very definite ideas, who wanted a diverse and varied curriculum to

Amos A. Lawrence, about 1870

include modern scientific studies as well as useful arts for large numbers of students. Fraser fostered the young faculty, fought for state and private funds, and scoured the nation for ideas to be incorporated into the great building that was later to bear his name. Finally, Fraser also fought with the faculty; he lost, and left it to Chancellor Marvin to finish University Hall. Marvin found the funds even while the state's and the nation's economies were collapsing; he also found time to plant a grove and build a fence to keep out the cows. And the students, almost literally a handful, have their faces clearly caught on a card the size of one's palm;

14

the tin-type portrait of Flora Richardson, the University's first valedictorian out of a class of four, is sadly crumpled. Four years later, the number of graduates had more than doubled; among them was Carrie Watson, who later lent her name to the new library, the central building of any university.

Buildings. In the first photo, North College is just barely visible in a space given over to grass, hill, and sky. With the camera moved up closer, this first building dominates the valley; when the law students have their picture taken, North College fills the frame. Trees then begin to compete with the structure for the eye's attention. To the south, not a shrub breaks the clean line of the horizon sloping away from Fraser with its hundred-foot-high towers and attendant chimneys. Students and teachers dot the foreground, where soon Chancellor Marvin, flush with $35,000 from the legislature, "had the grounds graded and caused grass to be sown." Other amenities had come: outside, gas-lamps and paved walkways; inside, fifty-four rooms "devoted to the work of instruction . . . in Chemistry, Physics, Natural Sciences, Mechanics, Engineering, and Drawing." There were also lecture halls, laboratories, a consulting library and places to "read in Greek, recite in Latin, and study the entire world." Often in the written reminiscences and the photos, that larger world was symbolized by the view from the top of the Hill, "stretching out on its own unbounded scale, unconfined." Inside, where professors shared with students a "contagious enthusiasm" for learning, and outside, too, the University was a place of vision.

Advertisement, *Junction City Union,* September 1, 1866

15

Standing on Oread hill, by the university, [I] have launch'd my view across broad expanses of living green, in every direction—I have again been most impress'd . . . with that feature of the topography of your western central world—that vast Something, stretching out on its own unbounded scale, unconfined, which there is in these prairies. . . .

Walt Whitman wrote of his 1879 visit to Lawrence, in *The Complete Writings of Walt Whitman*, 1902

The first building (North College), 1867

I was one among the fifty-five students of the first class of the university, and was proud of the fact. I struggled up the diagonal path to the summit of Mount Oread thinking of the wonders I was to do, read in Greek, recite in Latin and study the entire world. It was a tremendous undertaking, I knew, and I was inspired by it. . . . I stopped, gazed and dreamed—that was my college, stately red brick building, high arched windows and portly wooden doors, were to be mine. To the south was an unbroken prairie covered with grass more than knee high that waved and beckoned to the new college. Not a tree was on the hill, not a house nor an obstruction greater than the patch of sumac just east of the new building. It was a wondrous sight.

Lillian Robinson Leis recalling 1866, in the *Kansas City Star,* January 13, 1918

R. W. Oliver, chancellor, 1865–1867

It was with great difficulty that the location [of the University of Kansas] was secured here, and nothing saved us but the inducement of your fund.

Governor Charles Robinson, February 22, 1863, from a letter to Amos A. Lawrence of Boston, Massachusetts, who provided a $10,000 educational fund to Lawrence, Kansas, which was named in his honor; Kansas Collection, Spencer Research Library

The act organizing the University having passed in 1864, the Regents were formed in 1865, and they elected as their chairman and Chancellor of the University—with no teaching—the Rev. Mr. Oliver. . . . Mr. Oliver, with the help of his board, led the movement for a building through an amazingly complicated and persevering series of financial maneuvers. . . . He served the cause of higher education, first for his church, and later for the state, from March 1863 to December 1867 without pay, and left to take a pastorate in Nebraska.

Fred Ellsworth, ''Our Amazing Chancellors,'' *Alumni Magazine*

16

The youngest member of this faculty, unmarried, boyish in appearance, and with his laurels as honor student at Williams College still unfaded, was Francis Huntington Snow, who had been appointed to fill the chair of mathematics, as well as that of the natural sciences. It must have taken great faith for this clear-eyed young professor to have seen in this handful of young people the beginning of that strong institution which he so confidently predicted. . . . To these students, with the dark background of war and its hardships close behind them, Professor Snow with his buoyant kindly spirit, brought a fresh inspiration for intellectual culture. In his class-rooms, no one ever heard an impatient or a sarcastic expression. . . . It was, however, in the classes of zoology, botany, and geology that there was a contagious enthusiasm which made our work a real joy.

S. D. Alford, ''The First Five Years at Kansas University,'' in the *Graduate Magazine,* October 1909

Every enterprise has its difficulties to overcome, and the university is no exception to the rule. It is a great undertaking to establish a College, and no such institution can become a success without hard labor and patient waiting. I am not at all disheartened now, and look for better things next winter from a new legislature. . . .

Francis H. Snow, from a letter to his fiancée, Jane Aiken, March 25, 1868; University Archives

Francis H. Snow, professor of mathematics and sciences, 1866–1890; chancellor, 1890–1901; professor of natural history and director of the natural history museum, 1901–1908

Students, 1872

David H. Robinson,
professor of ancient
languages and
literatures, 1866–1895

19

Flora Richardson, valedictorian of the first graduating class of four students in 1873, was also one of the university's early graduate students. She received a Master of Arts degree in 1876, after her marriage to Osgood Colman.

Flora Richardson, about 1873

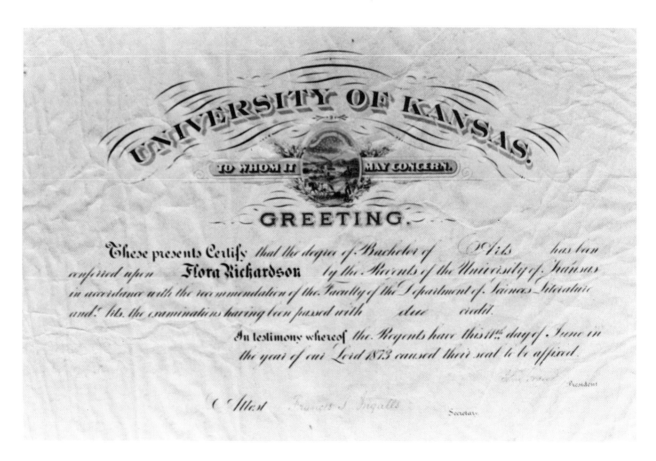

The first faculty, *Catalogue of the University of Kansas,* 1866

Elial J. Rice, professor of mental, moral science and belles lettres, 1866–1867

Elizabeth P. Leonard, professor of modern languages, drawing and painting, 1869–1874

Carrie Watson, librarian, 1878–1921, middle row, far right

Frederick E. Stimpson, professor
of chemistry and physics,
1871–1874

Byron Caldwell Smith, professor of Greek, 1872–1875

North College

I well remember the beautiful autumn day in 1879, when Father and I chose the buckboard to ride up the hill for my enrollment. Our choice of vehicle was of some importance, because "to ride up the hill" in those days depended somewhat upon the weather. In the dry season, a light carriage and one horse was sufficient; for rain, sleet, snow, and subsequent mud . . . but that is another story.

Agnes Emery, *Reminiscences of Early Lawrence,* 1954

North College with law students on steps, about 1890

North College, about 1900

Lawrence has already expended $100,000 upon the new university building, which is the largest and doubtless best planned college edifice in the United States. . . . One wing is nearly ready for the classes. The entire building is up and presents a most imposing appearance. It is 246 feet long, 100 wide and 100 high to the decks of the towers, and there does not seem to be a spare foot of room in it. The arrangement for the bestowal of the apparatus and cabinet is excellent, and the entire plan shows the good wisdom of General Fraser, who after visiting all the colleges of the East selected this plan as exactly filling the bill. We sincerely hope that enough ''lovers of learning'' will be found in our State legislature this winter to aid liberally this noble institution. . . .

Kansas Daily Tribune, December 16, 1871

Drawing for the new building, 1871

Now by the grace of God, we have a building nearly completed that has not its peer in the whole land. This building was not erected by the princely aid of a nobleman or millionaire, but it is the work of the people, the toiling thousands of our blood-bought Kansas. We accept it as a token of their liberality. The people have reason to rejoice with the faculty at what has been acomplished.

Chancellor John Fraser, at the public opening of the New Building, December 2, 1872

The building was first called the new building to distinguish it from the original building, North College. It was named University Hall in 1877 and renamed Fraser in 1897.

John Fraser, chancellor, 1867–1874

University Hall (Fraser), 1870s

Campus entrance and University Hall (Fraser), about 1879

It was Marvin's misfortune to face discouraging conditions. The financial collapse following the silver panic of 1873 affected the whole country for several years.

In Kansas, droughts and repeated invasions of grasshoppers caused hundreds of settlers to leave the state. Chancellor Marvin himself served willingly at a reduced salary, and induced other faculty members to do likewise.

Somehow, he got the Legislature to vote $35,000 to finish the grand new building, and from inferences in various writings of the time, it is apparent that he later got faculty salaries substantially increased. He had the grounds graded and caused grass to be sown. He installed a hedge fence on three sides of the main building and a stone wall with an iron gate on the other—to keep the wandering cows away.

Fred Ellsworth, "Our Amazing Chancellors," *Alumni Magazine*

James A. Marvin, chancellor, 1874–1883

29

University Hall (Fraser Hall), about 1882

CHAPTER TWO

Coming of Age

THE PHRASE "COMING OF AGE" suggests that during the two decades or so before the turn of the century, the University achieved a certain maturity, began to define its own special work, grew in size, and took on its characteristic appearance. The following photographs support these notions, but the camera is better at recording growth in size and identifying physical traits than it is at confirming maturity or sense of mission. True, the pharmacy demonstration and the engineering camp among the trees tell us that professional schools had evolved, as had Law, Education, Fine Arts, and a Graduate School offering degrees in fifteen areas. The students hearing the lecture from a skeleton in Professor Dyche's anatomy class may well be enrolled in the two-year course in medicine. Simeon Bell had given land for a teaching hospital near Kansas City, Kansas, but a medical school was some years away. Student life, too, was becoming more organized. Instead of individual portraits we have group pictures: eating clubs and mandolin clubs, Greek houses, a quartet. Professor Canfield, looking back at the first twenty-five years of the school, found no record of an athletic contest before 1880. Soon varsity sports were played on nationally standardized fields and courts with approved equipment and in appropriate uniforms. The lines of new McCook Field are cleanly etched against the scraggly brush in the foreground and the rather haphazard placement of buildings to the northwest. Some of the earlier roughness remains in the rutted mud of Oread Avenue but, on the whole, the Hill has taken on a settled look. Trees soften a bit the stark outlines and frame the buildings. The 100,000-volume library stacks already have some 20,000 items, among them books written by the emerging research faculty, magazines edited by student scientific and literary societies, and—by 1902—a humor magazine called *Automobile.*

The pictures, inevitably, reflect the nature of the age into which the University was coming. Within the frames there are more people, less space. Nowhere in America was the rate of population growth more dramatic than it was on the Prairie-Plains. Networks of railways, various homestead laws, new strains of winter wheat grown using new farming techniques and machinery made possible the settlement and cultivation of lands which, only a generation before, had been set aside as a permanent home for Native American Indians. Despite cycles of boom and bust, drought and depression, through Populist and Republican legislatures, Kansas' population swelled to near the million-and-a-half mark by 1900, competing for the first and last time with California. The University was competing less well, as Chancellor Lippincott pointed out in 1884 to the Regents: an average Kansas professor taught thirty-four students for twenty hours a week for an annual salary of $1,650. A California colleague taught nine students for nine hours and got $3,000. W.

H. Carruth would eventually be lured away to Stanford, but many of the faculty stayed to make names for themselves and the University: Blake in physics, Bailey in chemistry, Sayre in pharmacy, Green in law, Dyche in zoology, Hopkins in English. And the students came. Francis Snow had taught the original graduating class of four; when he turned the chancellorship over to Frank Strong in 1902, he could pass on, so to speak, nearly twelve hundred students. They were a varied lot, as their photographs show. Those on the field expeditions to Colorado—William Allen White among them—with their coarsely woven clothes and guns, look like frontier rowdies kept in check only by Professor Snow's butterfly net. The refined elegance of Kate Stephens, a student become professor of Greek, masks her caustic tongue, which, when she directed it at the Regents and the Chancellor, got her fired. Some Kansans—often newspaper editors— thought the Hill a bastion of privileged elitism. They were wrong, as a glance at the class of '95 will confirm. The largest number came from Kansas farms, but students' parents were engaged in some sixty different occupations. Over half of those who look out from these photographs were self-supporting.

The camera records not exclusiveness but necessity for smaller groups formed around varied interests—intellectual, professional, artistic, athletic, social. No longer can a camera get everyone into a single scene and still present individual faces distinctly. A little faster shutter speed has allowed the photographer to soften the stiffness of the earlier years and to stage something more informal. Students are now interrupted at the library, observed in their rooms, while the furnishings and paperwork of an administrative office are revealed. A finer lens catches the texture of cloth or boots; and, not meaning to, it includes many details that tell us about the larger forces at work in the world. Electric lines score the sky and link the old chemistry building and Snow Hall to some source of power, the same source that lights the incandescent bulbs in Spooner Library. The camera cannot, but Clifford Griffin, in his fine history of the University, can inform us that Blake Hall has high-voltage circuits and that fixtures were made of expensive copper and brass—not iron—so physics labs need not fear false magnetic fields. On Professor Bailey's new chemistry building, the chimneys and hoods indicate the intricate system of flues and fans necessary when science comes indoors. The stairs and stacks of Spooner are safely made of iron; a fire hydrant guards the new chemistry building. The University was ready for a future. True, the two original buildings—Old North and Fraser—would have to go, along with the chateau elegance of Blake and pinnacled Snow, which, too confidently, Governor Martin proclaimed to be "the home for all future time of the Department of Natural History." A half-century later Fowler changed its name to Flint; the new chemistry building, Bailey, lost its chimneys and became the School of Education. The old chemistry building was finally razed, but its stair-stepped Dutch gables still echo in the west façade of Spooner. In the final photograph the site is ready for the ornate "Venetian Romanesque" of Dyche. Shunning uniformity, the buildings mingle many cultures. *Oread eclectic* has become the identifying pattern, as has another pattern: three new structures have been built by the state, three by private gifts. The six define the curve of Oread Avenue into Jayhawk Boulevard and point westward to further growth.

Faculty group, 1881–1882 *Left to right, top row:* Lehman, Summerfield, Miller, H. H. S. Smith, Patrick; *second row:* Spring, Chancellor Marvin, Green; *third row:* Snow, Canfield, Schlegel, Robinson, F. O. Marvin; *bottom:* Carruth, Williams, Gleed

In the early days of the University under the administration of General Fraser, Dr. James Marvin, and Dr. Lippincott, the institution was simply a college and nothing more, and for many years the majority of the students belonged to the so-called preparatory department. The faculty was very small, and the salaries smaller still. The brilliant men of the faculty, accordingly, were restive, and could not resist the temptation of putting their ears to the ground, to hear, if perchance, an invitation to better positions in other and older institutions might not come their way. Professor Spring was among the first to receive a message. Williams College called him, and he accepted the call. Professor Nichols was the next to go. Cornell captured him. James H. Canfield was taken, but with reluctance on his part. Nebraska caught him with a five-thousand-dollar bait. Professor Arthur Canfield was interviewed by President Angell of Michigan, who said to the Professor, ''Come up higher,'' and the Professor went. Leland Stanford carried away three others. Shame on Leland Stanford. Everybody knew that the big California institution had vast amounts of money in reserve, but it was not so well known that that institution was in need of brains, and in order to get a superior quality of the same, had to come to Kansas to secure them.

E. Miller, *Graduate Magazine*, January 1905

33

34

Cora M. Downs, first woman regent

Several months ago I had some correspondence with you in relation to the propriety of appointing a woman as Regent of the State University. . . . I have long been of the opinion that all of our State institutions where females are educated or cared for should have a woman as a member of the boards representing such institutions.

This policy no doubt at first will be—while it receives the endorsement of some—by many severely criticised. Yet I believe it is right, and if right, Kansas can afford to adopt it. At all events I am willing to take the initial steps.

Letter to Cora Downs from Governor John St. John, December 21, 1881; quoted in *Kansas Alumni,* October 1981

William C. Spangler, class of '83, served as regent, 1888–1893, as acting chancellor, 1889–1890, and as vice chancellor, 1900–1901

First chemistry building, opened in 1883

Snow Hall, dedicated in 1886

Professor Snow and students, on a collecting expedition in 1889 *Left to right:* W. A. White, Harry Riggs, Frank Craig, Ed Franklin, Vernon Kellogg, A. L. Wilmoth *(in door),* Schuyler Brewster *(at side),* Herbert Hadley *(below),* Jennie Sutliff, Eva Fleming, Nellie Franklin, the Burro, W. S. Franklin, Helen Sutliff, Professor Snow

We meet, to-day, to formally celebrate another step in the growth and progress of the State University— to dedicate this beautiful building, the home for all future time, of the department of natural history. Very properly the building is to bear the name of the learned, devoted and enthusiastic teacher to whose energy, industry and zeal the state is indebted for treasures that are gathered within its walls. I discharge a very pleasant duty, gentlemen of the board of regents, when in the name of the State I commit to your keeping this stately edifice.

Governor John A. Martin, at the dedication of Snow Hall, quoted in the *Weekly University Courier,* November 19, 1886

Spooner Library, completed in 1894

The Spooner library building was built from money left in 1891 by William B. Spooner of Boston. He left, by will, to Kansas university and Oberlin college in Ohio each the sum of $91,618. The donor was an uncle of Chancellor F. H. Snow, the present head of Kansas university, and a liberal patron of educational institutions. He appreciated the work done by his nephew, and for that reason remembered the school of which he is now the head by the splendid legacy. Two years ago this winter the Legislature of the State decided that the money thus bequeathed should be used for the erection of a library building and for the building for a home for the chancellor of the university.

Kansas City Times, October 10, 1894

On the Spooner Library steps, about 1896

This trip of '89 was the most famous of several Estes Park excursions from the University, in which students and faculty joined. It represented more to me than any other ten weeks in my life—more in the way of stimulation—spiritual, emotional, physical— than anything that ever happened. . . . I am quite sure I was more of a person for the heart interest that developed on the trip, which was, in itself, a liberal education.

William Allen White, from a letter describing the 1889 collecting expedition to Colorado; University Archives

Reference division, Spooner Library

Spooner Library stacks

1890 faculty group *Left to right, standing:* W. C. Stevens, L. E. Sayre, Olin Templin, L. I. Blake, C. G. Dunlap, D. H. Robinson, E. M. Hopkins, A. M. Wilcox, F. W. Blackmar, E. H. S. Bailey, H. B. Newson, E. C. Franklin, F. O. Marvin, E. F. Engel, S. R. Boyce; *seated:* F. H. Hodder, Vernon Kellogg, L. L. Dyche, Ephraim Miller, Frances Schlegel, W. H. Carruth, F. H. Snow, Cora Parker, A. G. Canfield, S. W. Williston, G. B. Penney, M. W. Sterling

38

Like every similar institution, this University met with its share of delays and difficulties and disappointments. But under the leadership of courageous and energetic men it has pushed its way to the point where it has become the pride of the state, and where its future, we trust, is secure. . . . It has more than thirty teachers, and among them are men of national reputation, whom some of the older and larger universities would be very glad to borrow from you. It has a large outfit of the appliances for teaching the sciences according to the modern methods. In a word, it is furnishing excellent instruction in that variety of work now expected of good classical and scientific colleges, schools of pharmacy and schools of law. . . . It is no exaggeration to say, that in its twenty-five years of existence this University has made more progress than Harvard College made in two centuries from its foundation.

From 1891 commencement address by J. B. Angell, president of the University of Michigan, in *Quarter-Centennial History of the University of Kansas, 1866-1891*

William H. Carruth, professor of German and English, 1879–1913

As a boy he [Chancellor Snow] had raised chickens, and his fondness for them remained. . . . Since his son Frank liked chickens and rabbits, too, Snow arranged to have a pen and hutches placed under the roomy front porch of the Chancellor's house. Visiting his pets under the porch, young Frank was sometimes amused to overhear, along with the cackling of his hens, comments by women who called on his mother and who thought it an impropriety to keep chickens in such a place.

Clyde K. Hyder, *Snow of Kansas*, 1953

Chancellor's residence, from 1894 to 1939, 1345 Louisiana

Kate Stephens, professor
of Greek language and literature,
1878–1885

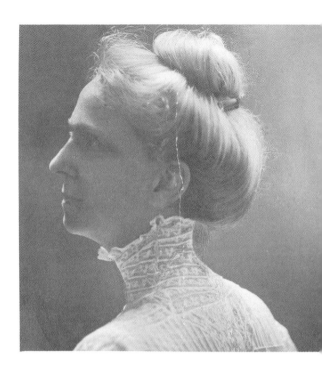

Hannah Oliver, professor of Latin, 1890–1931

Physics building (Blake Hall), opened in 1895

My predecesor had a single clerk, whose chief duty it was to record the grades and receive the tuition and laboratory fees of the students. . . . Chancellor Lippincott had no stenographer and was compelled to write every letter by hand in the good old fashioned way. During the late administration there were, in place of the single clerk of the 80's, a Treasurer and Purchasing Agent, a Registrar, a Private Secretary, a Stenographer and a ''guide,'' all of whom gave their entire time to the executive service.

From an address by Francis H. Snow, chancellor from 1890 to 1901, at the inauguration of Chancellor Frank Strong; in the *Graduate Magazine*, November 1902

The physics building was officially named Blake Hall in 1898 in honor of Lucien I. Blake, professor of physics, astronomy, and electrical engineering from 1887 to 1906.

Chancellor Snow and his private secretary, Vernon Kellogg, about 1891

Pharmacy demonstration, 1891   The hatless gentleman on the far left is Professor Sayre, dean of the School of Pharmacy

1894 law class   The bearded gentleman in the front row is Supreme Court Justice D. M. Valentine, who was a part-time lecturer in the Law School from 1894 to 1898; to his left are Dean J. W. Green and Professor S. A. Riggs.

Professor Dyche and anatomy class, 1890s

LEWIS LINDSAY DYCHE

TRAVELING COSTUME.

HARPOONING A WALRUS IN ARCTIC SEAS.

SLEEPING COSTUME.

KILLING THE HARPOONED WALRUS.

IN HIS FAMOUS LECTURES:

1. Greenland and the Arctic Regions.

2. Scenes from the Land of the Midnight Sun.

3. The Arctic Highlanders and the Problem of the Pole.

———

400 STEREOPTICON VIEWS.

Naturalist and Explorer

Promotional poster for Dyche's public lectures

E. M. Hopkins, professor of English, and class, about 1899

Class of 1895, on steps of Snow Hall

Every student should seek plain, nutritious food, well prepared, served at regular intervals, and never taken in haste nor in the presence of books.

University of Kansas Catalogue, 1882–1883

Student room, about 1891

The life of the students has never dominated that of the town, as it has often done when institutions are located in little country villages. Furthermore, the students have never been separated from the larger community, as in colleges where the dormitory system prevails. They have not lived by themselves apart, but have been scattered and swallowed up in the homes of the city. The student body, therefore, has never felt itself to be a wholly separate world. . . .

Arthur G. Canfield, "Student Life in K. S. U."; in *Quarter-Centennial History of the University of Kansas, 1866–1891*

By uniting in clubs, and boarding themselves, students may reduce their expenses one half.

University of Kansas Catalogue, 1867–1868

Boarding Club, 1895–1896

Psi Upsilon, 1886–1887

Kappa Kappa Gamma, 1891

The social life of the University cannot well be considered apart from the fraternities, for it has centered in them. . . . As a rule each fraternity has planned to have two considerable social events during the year. These have usually taken the form of evening parties, with dancing and refreshments. More rarely have these events taken the shape of formal dinners or suppers with toasts and perhaps some musical or literary features. Unusual activity in social life is indicated by the frequency of informal hops or other parties. Only rarely and among a small circle of students has this social activity amounted to dissipation or invaded the precincts of the University building.

Arthur G. Canfield, "Student Life in K. S. U."; in *Quarter-Centennial History of the University of Kansas, 1866–1891*

Beta Theta Pi quartet, 1899

Mandolin Club

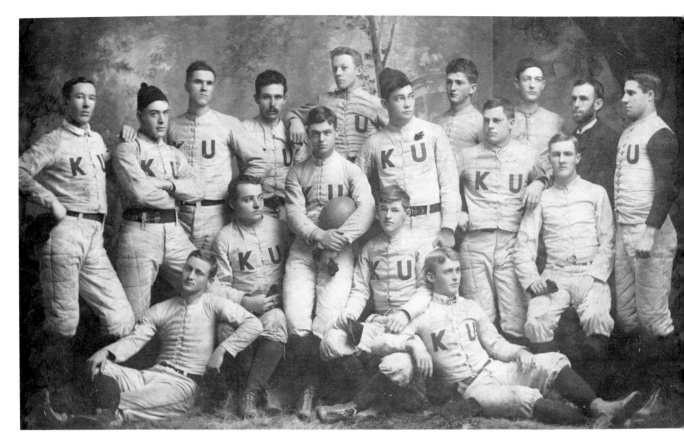

First football squad, 1891   The coach *(top row in dark suit)* is Professor E. M. Hopkins of the English department

Tennis Club, 1892   *Left to right, standing:* J. Bassett, Hattie
Ayres, May Gardner, Genevieve Howland Chalkley, Grace
Colwell, Jeannette Wheeler; *seated:* Madge Bullene, Anna
Drake, Edith Snow, Louise Towne, Grace Poff

There has been no regular rivalry between the University and other colleges, and contests with other colleges have been few and far between. This apathy in athletics has been remarked very frequently in the University papers. . . . Naturally all our contests with other colleges have been in base ball, until last fall, but I do not find a record of any contest at all before 1880. . . . Foot ball as a scientific game was never introduced in the University till last fall, when it created a great deal of enthusiasm and did much to stimulate a general interest in out-door sports.

Arthur G. Canfield, ''Student Life in K. S. U.''; in *Quarter-Centennial History of the University of Kansas, 1866–1891*

Football team, 1893

Baseball team, 1894

1895 football squad

A grand stand to seat 1,000 people is well under way, . . . this is in the northwest corner and will be painted crimson. A board fence is being built around the graded part of the grounds. At the northeast corner will be the entrance, ticket office and dressing rooms. Hitching racks will be put up inside the fence, a good walk made from the street to the gate, and, in fact, everything pertaining to a first-class athletic field will be in shape when the University opens.

University Courier, August 1, 1892

McCook Field, about 1893

When we finally evolved basket ball we played it with peach baskets for goals. The girls played it in high-heeled shoes. They wore their bustles. It was a mess.

James Naismith, quoted in the *Kansas City Times*, January 10, 1931

Every one who is at all interested in athletics is now talking basket ball. Yet it does not stop here. Those who hitherto have manifested no interest in any sports of skill and strength seem now to be enthusiastic over the new game. It is talked at the club; it is discussed in the corridors; it is practiced and played in the gymnasium and on the campus. Even the professors have become actively interested in the game and are giving their time of recreation over to this pastime.

Kansas University Weekly, December 10, 1898

First basketball team, 1898–1899   Dr. James Naismith, the inventor of basketball, is in the back row, far right

Cheerleaders at McCook Field, 1899

No one can well doubt the vigorous loyalty of the student body to the University when he hears the thunder of the college yell sent up from the foot-ball or base-ball field. The existence of the yell itself is a proof of that spirit; one common sentiment of love and pride and exultation seeks expression in one common form of words—"Rock Chalk, Jay Hawk, K. U."

Arthur G. Canfield, "Student Life in K. S. U."; in *Quarter-Centennial History of the University of Kansas, 1866–1891*

Fowler Shops (Flint Hall), opened in 1899

If I were asked to name the principal features which characterized the growth of the University of Kansas during its fifth executive administration, I should mention the following: . . . The entire exclusion of the Preparatory Department. . . . The increase in enrollment of students from 505 to 1154. . . . The enlargement of the Faculties of instruction from 34 to 79 members. . . . The receipt of private gifts to such an extent that the University of Kansas has received from private sources a larger per cent of its educational plant than any other State University. . . . The erection of six new buildings,—three by the State and three by the generosity of Wm. B. Spooner and George A. Fowler. . . . The addition of eight acres on Oread Avenue to

the University campus, and twelve more acres for an athletic field, those gifts having been bestowed by Charles Robinson, Wm. B. Spooner, and John J. McCook. . . . I look forward with confidence to a period in the life time of many within the hearing of my voice to-day, when by public generosity aided by private munificence, Mt. Oread shall be covered with educational structures, faultlessly planned, devoted to the various departments of science and the humanities, thronged with thousands of students from this and other states, intent upon the greatest possible development of the immortal mind and soul.

From an address by Francis H. Snow, former chancellor, at the inauguration of Chancellor Frank Strong; in the *Graduate Magazine,* November 1902

New chemistry building (Bailey Hall), opened in 1900

On arriving in Lawrence the new instructor is likely to receive one of two distinct impressions, if he attempts to climb Mt. Oread on foot: if the day be hot he wonders why there are no trolley cars; if it be rainy he wonders why there are not more side-walks. As he toils up the hill, balancing himself on a three-inch curbstone to avoid the mud on either side, he first notices the iron standing tower with its flaring class numerals, and in the distance, North College rising in bleak isolation; he wonders with sinking heart if these buildings are the University of Kansas, but remembers the descriptions in the bulletin and has the courage to proceed. As he reaches the summit, faces the other way and sees the real University, he feels a glad reaction and his spirits rise suddenly to an unwonted height. The wide sweep of the view, the exhilarating air, the noble buildings, but above all the possibilities of development stimulate the imagination. . . . It requires no prophet to foretell a time when the entire hill shall be cultivated with the highest art of the landscape gardener, and crowned with buildings from end to end. . . . But even as he thus muses he treads on a loose end of the plank walk and a jet of muddy water spurts over his clothing. . . .

Graduate Magazine, December 1903

About 1900

1902

CHAPTER THREE

A New Century

THE INAUGURATION of Frank Strong in 1902 meant the University would have but one chancellor for nearly two decades of the new century. By the end of World War I, his hair had turned white, but he was a man as strong in nature as in name. Up until the eve of the Great War, general prosperity and a fairly compliant legislature allowed expansion on the Hill and extension beyond to places this photographic history does not reach: the medical college in Kansas City, guidance and improvement of the state's primary and secondary education, the Geological Survey, faculty chemists and engineers on "Industrial Fellowships" in regional manufacturing and business firms, 1500 students enrolled in correspondence courses, and a university public relations department that sent out news and photos like many shown here. These were some of the ways the University under Strong tried both to influence and to keep "in touch with the great current" of state and national life. Erasmus Haworth's hope that development of solar power might free the nation from "coal barons" and "transportation monopolists" reminds us that this was the era of Teddy Roosevelt's trust-busting crusades. Professor Bailey's chemical tests for the purity of foodstuffs were devised in a climate created by such muckraking journalism as Upton Sinclair's exposure of the Chicago meat-packing industry. More and more the University looked outward. The ease and economy of rail travel brought to

many Kansas communities performances by the orchestral and choral groups of George Penny and Charles Skilton, sometimes a solo by the renowned Hungarian-born professor of violin, Geza-Dome. Interurban trains also allowed students and alums to follow the football team to games which, in the minds of men like Chancellor Strong and President of the Faculty Carruth, had become less amateur than befit the University. But athletics had assumed an importance not to be relinquished. The "seasons" had taken on new adjectives: football, basketball, baseball, and track. Already, in the 1904 master plan for the campus drawn up by the Kansas City architect George Kessler, a gymnasium with bleachers and a large stadium flank the gateway to the University.

In 1902 a camera perched on the old iron water-tower and pointed south flattens a bit the outline of the Hill where the tile-red roofs form a nearly continuous if jagged line from east to west. Seen from the northwest, the University presents an isolated but imposing cluster that, by the summer before the war, has become rather peacefully bucolic. Take away the cowboy and his cows, add a campanile in memorial to another war, and the view has changed little to this day—right down to the dandelions gone to seed. Within, the campus has a more urban look, particularly the photo of the electric streetlights, trolley, trash can, and fire hydrant. Dean Marvin has a telephone. Automobiles compete with buggies for parking space on May

Day, 1908. Dyche's panorama of North American mammals, first shown at Chicago's Columbian Exposition of 1893, now has a home; outside, odd stone mammals await installation. The Law School, long the private fiefdom of Dean "Uncle Jimmy" Green, adds a Grecian temple to the campus. Engineering, the most successful of the new schools during these years, gets its own building; innovative interior walls made it strong enough to last, no doubt, into the twenty-first century. Marvin's "Collegiate Tudor" echoed the lines of the new gym, Robinson, where there was now sufficient space for banquets or basketball. Dr. Naismith's original peach-basket has given way to an iron hoop on the backboard. The stern formality of Erasmus Haworth belies the warm heartiness of a man students called "Daddy." Across from Haworth Hall the stark, neo-Egyptian administration building awaits completion after the return to peace. For the duration of the war, new buildings will be temporary. The barracks shown here were under construction less than a month before the armistice was signed. Off camera, in a dozen finished barracks east of McCook Field, influenza had broken out. Seven hundred and fifty students were down; thirty-two died.

May Day rites and military drills on the lawn east of Fraser Hall suggest something of the contrasts and changes of the new century. These photographs, like most in the book, will repay one's perusal, perhaps with magnifying glass in hand. At the far end of the drill-line, Myers Hall, home of the Kansas Bible Chair, appears; the clock on Blake tells us the camera snapped at 5:35 on the afternoon of May 1, 1908; some cowboy hats and bowlers are sprinkled among the mortarboards of the Class of '05. Annually since 1891, freshmen and sophomore men had fought over class flags atop a Maypole in the May Day scrap. This vestige of "pioneer rowdyism" had grown so brutal by 1904 that the following year a mock funeral effectively buried the custom, and a more genteel observation of May Day evolved. Student behavior outside the classroom was more closely monitored as a policy of *in loco parentis* emerged. A "women's adviser," forerunner to the dean of women, was appointed; student living groups were more strictly supervised; the Tango Club's sensuous dancing was banned in 1913. Nineteen-fourteen brought war to Europe but no immediate dramatic change to the University: Professor Griffith's students of 1915 paint life studies rather than roll bandages; his children pick daisies on the hill to the west. America declared war in April 1917. By May, before the end of classes, some five hundred students had left to enter military service or war work. A sympathetic Faculty Senate voted those students the full semester credit. Of those who stayed on the Hill, more than half the male students formed the University Regiment, took military courses, drilled (with mock rifles made in Fowler Shops) under Professor—"Colonel"—Briggs of the German department. The "rising whistle" now sounded at 6:30 A.M. Women students held a mass protest meeting, but were nevertheless included in compulsory physical training. The physical education department swelled in size. Concentration on regular study was very difficult; the faculty was decimated; dress became more somber. But Frank Strong's fear "of an almost total paralysis and disintegration of the institution" was not realized. The photograph of the half-razed Old North College might have been taken on the battlefields of France, but it wasn't. Old ground was being cleared for the University's first dormitory.

The position of any university carries with it great responsibility to the state and to society in general. Particularly is this true of a state university. It is created by the state. It is maintained in great part by general taxation. It must be, then, in a peculiar manner a servant of the commonwealth and must fulfill all the functions that such a relation requires. It ought to be the center of the intellectual life of the state. It should influence every department of life in the commonwealth, and must therefore keep itself in close touch with the great current of life in the state and out.

From Chancellor Strong's inauguration address, in the *Graduate Magazine,* November 1902

Museum of Natural History (Dyche Museum), 1902

The entire ornamental stone job of the Dyce [*sic*] Museum including the animals was executed by Joseph Roblado Frazee . . . a master carver and sculptor. No models were used for the figures; a stone was set up on a block, a few (to me) meaningless marks were made on it and then the mallet and chisel in Mr. Frazee's hands started at the top and worked down, to free the figure from its encasing stone.

A. Tommasini, from a letter in the University Archives

Carving gargoyles for Natural History Museum

Inauguration day, October 17, 1902 *Left to right (standing on the first three steps):* Ex-chancellor Francis H. Snow, Governor William E. Stanley, President Arthur T. Hadley of Yale, Regent Thomas M. Potter, Chancellor Frank Strong

Music faculty, 1903–4 *Left to right:* C. E. Hubach, Jean Bowersock, Charles Sanford Skilton, Harriet Greissinger, Carl A. Preyer

Class of 1905 on the steps of Blake Hall

Baseball team, 1903

Returning from the Nebraska game, 1908

Varsity basketball squad

The relatively sound tone and conditions of sports at the University of Kansas during the past season should make it possible to take a dispassionate view of the agitation on this subject which is stirring the entire country. It is not probable that a public indignation meeting, presided over by a member of the faculty, will again be held, as was done five years ago, to denounce a lifelong friend of students and student sports because he declared that roughness and professionalism were too prevalent in our games. The same conviction has now become practically universal, and the only division of opinion regarding football has become whether the game shall be cured or killed.

W. H. Carruth, from "The Athletic Situation," in the *Graduate Magazine,* January 1906

Architect's plan for the university, 1904

Chancellors Lippincott, Strong, and Snow, 1906

Green Hall (now Lippincott), dedicated in 1905

About 1906

The University was Gov. Robinson's comforting
love and joy. In its great prosperity to-day he would
feel well repaid for all his labor and anxieties. . . .
Truly, what a marvel God hath wrought! He saved
us from the border men and slavery in the days of
our small beginnings, when for a time we seemed to
be swinging in the balance, and He has led us
forward in our days of quiet prosperity and peace.
We are always thankful to those who aided in our
days of dire uncertainty. Let us give thanks to Gov.
Robinson that he showed unfailing devotion to his
pet scheme, for providing for a university for the
youth of Kansas, to my nephew Frank B. Lawrence,
for endeavoring to carry out his uncle's wishes, and
to the Chancellor for his untiring zeal to accomplish
what they had begun. The magnificent Robinson
Hall is an enduring memorial in stone of what has
been done. . . .

Sara T. D. Robinson, from a letter read at the dedication of Robinson
Hall; University Archives

Robinson Hall, dedicated in 1906

Gymnastics in Robinson gym, 1911

Engineering building (Marvin Hall), opened in 1908

Geology and mining building (Haworth Hall), opened in 1909

The work which the University is
doing for the State, other than
that of training its students, is
growing rapidly with experience.
Many of the members of the
faculty of the School of Engineering are actively at work on
research problems relating to the
strength of materials, oil and gas
investigations, sanitary questions
connected with water supply and
drainage, road materials, mine
explosions, fuels, the technology
of glass and cement manufacturing, electric power problems, etc.

F. O. Marvin, from a letter inviting
engineering alumni to the dedication of Marvin
and Haworth halls, February 1910; University
Archives

Frank O. Marvin, dean of the School of Engineering

It [the energy of the sun] is so
tremendously great that when
measured by any standard within
the comprehension of man we
are lost in the enumeration. . . .
If a man has intelligence,—if he
understand nature, if modern
man is so far superior to his
ancient ancestors as we love to
boast,—why does not man go
directly to nature for heat to
warm his dwellings, for light to
dispel the darkness, for power to
propel his machinery and to
carry on his commerce? Then we
would have no coal barons for no
one would use coal; then we
would have no transportation
monopolists, for energy would be
available for all. . . .

Erasmus Haworth, from "A New Building
and the Future," in the *Graduate Magazine*,
March 1910

Erasmus Haworth, professor of geology, mineralogy, and mining

69

Phi Kappa Psi fraternity house, 1140 Louisiana, about 1910

The Phi Kappa Psi house was designed by William A. Griffith, professor of drawing and painting.

Smith rooming house, 1145 Louisiana, about 1910

What is the matter with K.U.? . . . The May Pole "scrap" is gone, or emasculated into "Ring around the Rosy;" the junior prom and the senior reception are as tame as a pink tea in an Old Ladies' Home; even our old yell is now sung instead of shouted.

Frank R. Whitzel, in the *Graduate Magazine,* January 1911

I, for one, am proud that the University is growing in this way as in all others, and has evolved past the stage of pioneer rowdyism which once went for enthusiasm. . . . That the University is today an institution of the kind which breeds respect for dignity and gentleness, is something to take pride in, and not to deplore. . . . Every one who was at K.U. in the days of the May-pole scrap, and like institutions, knows that those things did a great deal of real harm to the University's reputation over the state and even farther afield. . . .

Estelle Riddle Dodge, in the *Graduate Magazine,* June 1911

Our University life is after all very plain. Whatever may be said about the social indulgence of this class or that, or the misguided extravagances of one or another, our general body lives a sober and sedate and on the whole a rather work-a-day existence. We have our holidays, to be sure, when pleasure becomes a private enterprise, or our special occasions when we try to lose our heads enthusiastically over athletics, and make pleasure a public business with definite gain in view. But generally our centralizing interest is work or the civic affairs of our own organization. We try to snatch profit from what pleasures we have in common and rarely enjoy our delights in community.

But in the last four years we have a new custom—a real gala day, a May festival occasion.

Margaret Lynn, in the *Graduate Magazine,* June 1911

May Day fete, 1908

May Day fete, 1911

Commencement regatta, 1911

Nightshirt parade

Streetcars on campus

The legislature and the governor have again handed the University a meal ticket with holes punched in it. The biggest hole is the one where the Board had put down $250,000 for the central section of the Administration building. . . . The most serious mutilation of the ticket was the punching of $76,670 from the maintenance. . . . The total reduction from the requests of the Board was $431,670. . . . So much for figures. What do they mean? Can the University get along on the income granted?

As regards maintenance the University can get along perhaps as well as in the past biennium, but it can not attempt the extensions of its work nor raise its salary standings in keeping with the progress of universities generally.

Graduate Magazine, March 1915

Administration building (east wing of Strong Hall), 1911

Engineering banquet in Robinson gym, 1912   Professor Haworth and Dean Marvin are seated in the center foreground

Law School banquet, 1912   Chancellor Strong and Law School Dean James W. Green are standing at center front

Mu Phi Epsilon music sorority, 1912

University orchestra, 1913–1914

Dean Charles Skilton at Fraser Hall organ, 1915

80

Professor E. H. S. Bailey

In accordance with a law passed by our legislature at its last session, the department of chemistry of the University and that of the State Agricultural College began the crusade for pure food more than a year ago. . . .

They have tested the various packing house products for preservatives; . . . they have traced the ''pure maple syrup'' to the cane brakes of Louisiana; jams and jellies have had their compositions so exposed that if they had not been already red as aniline colors could make them, they would have blushed to acknowledge that no fruit whatever had been used in their manufacture.

E. H. S. Bailey, ''The Practical Side of Some Scientific Work in the University,'' in the *Graduate Magazine*, November 1906

When I first went to the University of Kansas, it was aloof from the people. The preachers hated it because it taught evolution. The politicians disliked it because they suspected that free trade was advocated in the class room when Kansas was over-whelmingly Republican. Chancellor Oliver, Chancellor Marvin and Chancellor Lippincott had been preachers, so the unregenerated disliked the University because of its unction and the religious flavor which they thought the preacher-chancellors gave it. Chancellor Snow began to popularize the University, but under the direction of Frank Strong a dozen services connecting the University with the people were established. It took deep root in the Kansas heart. That extension of popular state services I think is one of the chief contributions which Frank Strong made to the University of Kansas. He brought the University to the Kansas people and popularizing gave it academic dignity as well.

William Allen White, in the *Graduate Magazine,* October 1934

Pottery class, 1913

Psychology laboratory, 1913

Professor William A. Griffith's drawing class, 1915

Senior women's basketball team 1919 Wealthy Babcock,
front row, second from left

Daisy Hill, 1915   Professor Griffith's children

Adelaide Steger, physical education instructor, 1918–1923

Net ball

H. G. Green, janitor in the Fowler Shops

SATC headquarters force

Of the University of Kansas men in the army and navy twenty-seven are members of the faculty and are absent from the University on leave of absence for the duration of the war. Additional faculty members are giving their time exclusively to other war work, such as the service of Doctor James Naismith and P. A. F. Appleboom in Y.M.C.A. work in France, Dean Olin Templin and Miss Elizabeth Sprague in the food administration office at Washington and other instructors in government laboratories and on munition plant construction work, and in other services. . . . As an example of how thoroughly war needs raided the University, the department of psychology lost its entire faculty, with the exception of assistant instructors. Its three professors were taken by the army to make psychological tests in examining recruits for aviation and other special work. Seven members of the engineering faculty were taken and the physical education department lost five of its faculty. Only this summer five more of the faculty of the department of French have been taken. Of forty-two graduates in the engineering classes of 1918, not one could attend commencement exercises to receive his diploma.

Graduate Magazine, June 1918

Student Army Training Corps battalion on parade, 1918

SATC barracks

Women's war work

I shall leave the administration of the University with regret but with great satisfaction. It has been my lot to see the institution grow under my hand from a small college of 1200 students to a real university with about 4000 students. I have seen the body of teachers and administrators in the University increase from 80 to 311. . . . During my incumbency I have seen eighteen new buildings and additions erected, the last of them being the west wing and central portion of the building for administration and the College of Liberal Arts, a building of great size and great beauty. I have seen the library increase from 37,000 volumes to 125,000 volumes and the scope of the work of the University greatly increased by the addition of many schools and departments. I have had the great pleasure also to graduate about 5,500 of the 7,540 graduates of the institution.

Chancellor Frank Strong, letter of resignation to the Board of Administration, in the *Graduate Magazine,* October 1919

Students training with wooden rifles   Fred Ellsworth is second from the right

SATC induction ceremony Chancellor Strong is seated third from the right

Old North College of Kansas University, the trysting place of years, is soon to be razed. No longer will couples sit on the south stairs of the building and watch the lazy moon creep up over the housetops east of the hill. The old square tower, high above the surrounding lands, will house no more youthful romances. The sounds of the fine arts school, which for several years has been held in the building, will no more shatter the peace of the slopes. The building, the oldest of the college halls at KU, is to be torn down. . . .

Kansas City Star, January 13, 1918

Ruins of old North College, 1918

CHAPTER FOUR

Between the Wars

THE FIRST TWO PHOTOGRAPHS in this section appear to be of different universities: one is older, mellowed, maybe an eastern college; the other is brand-new, up-to-date, and rather business-like. The first, taken at 10:30 on an early spring morning in 1920, captures the warm texture of brick sidewalks and stone walls of quietly ornate buildings. Surely here, as Chancellor Lindley assured parents, a student could learn while living simply, morally, and wholesomely, without an automobile. Around the corner is a bright new concrete boulevard with plenty of parking in the shade of newly planted American elms. The war over, the barracks gone, the administration building finally finished, the older campus moves to the background. An aerial photographer excludes altogether Fraser, Dyche, Spooner, Blake, Old Snow, even Green. The stadium, built as a memorial to those lost in the war and dedicated on Armistice Day, 1922, is already too small for the crowd that will come to watch the 1923 championship team. With the help of a "Million Dollar Drive" among private supporters and alumni, the stadium's familiar U-shape will be filled out in time for those who will watch Glenn Cunningham run. Fast cameras can now catch bodies in motion, women hurdlers, water splashing from Potter's pond or reflecting the image of Fraser Hall in a puddle in front of the wooden-frame Commons cafeteria. Old Snow Hall, its vines masking serious flaws, hides the new library where the formida-

ble Carrie Watson imposes studious quiet. Raymond Nichols prefers to study in his room. Chancellor Nichols, in his vivid introduction to this volume, gives the lie to the notion that the fun-loving Roaring Twenties much affected student life. Still, the sons and daughters of earlier students who formed a "Second Generation Club" look a little brasher than their parents had. That was 1928. The University was "between wars" and on the threshold of Depression and Dust Bowl.

In the fifth year of his chancellorship, Ernest H. Lindley, a psychologist and a "courtly" and "genial" man, got himself fired for insubordination—but only briefly—by outgoing Governor Davis, acting as head of the State Board of Administration. Reinstated by the new governor, and working with a reconstituted Board of Regents, Lindley served for nineteen years. Like Strong before him, he presided over two very diverse decades. How buildings got built tell us something of the difference. In the twenties, thousands of alumni and friends donated nearly $700,000 to help build Memorial Stadium and the Memorial Union. This was a time of great growth for both the Alumni and Endowment associations. State funds were also generous. Corbin Hall, named for Alberta Corbin, professor of German, who led the statewide legislative campaign for women's dormitories, opened in 1923. The new library brought space for the overflowing collection in Spooner, and it also brought the Hill's first

Administration building (Strong Hall), finally finished in early 1920s

First aerial view of KU, 1921

The University is using every effort to keep among students a fine spirit of democracy, to concentrate students' attention upon serious study and healthful recreation, and to hold to a minimum practices fraught with moral risks. . . . You can help much by making it clear to your sons and daughters that their part is to live simply, honestly and wholesomely while in the University. For this they do not need a car.

Chancellor E. H. Lindley, in letter to parents, 1922; quoted in the *Graduate Magazine*

The setting of the college surprised us, for, if there was one thing we had expected more than another, it was that Kansas would prove absolutely flat. Yet here we were on a mountain top—at least they call it Mount Oread—with the valley of the Kaw River below, and what seemed to be the whole of Kansas spread around about, like a vast panoramic mural decoration for the university.

Julian Street, *Collier's*, October 24, 1914

"Collegiate Gothic," a style modified for Hoch Auditorium and new Snow Hall westward up the boulevard. Hoch was also modified so that it could accommodate not only convocations and musical and theatrical performances but Dr. F. C. "Phog" Allen's fine basketball teams. The opening of new Snow in 1930 made possible the razing of Old Snow—the delapidated, rat-infested, firetrap that housed parasitology and bacteriology. In the thirties, public funds, like the weather, dried up. Buildings came now from a single benefactor, Mrs. Elizabeth Watkins: two women's residence halls, another for nurses, a student hospital rivaled only, it was said, by the one at Berkeley; she gave her home as a chancellor's residence, and 26,000 acres then in the heart of the Dust Bowl but soon to become once again productive.

The popular images of the Great Depression—idle factories, discouraged faces, soup lines, people on the road or on the dole—come from newsreel and government and news photographers. People neither ask nor pay to have their misery recorded. Perhaps that's why no photos have surfaced to clearly connect University life to those popular images of economic and political dislocation. The students dressed in rags and grinning for Hobo Day in 1934 are for the moment light-hearted while observing a custom from more prosperous times. The continuity of life on the Hill between the twenties and the thirties appears more stable in these pictures than it really was. Enrollment dropped and funding was slashed. Most students now combined study with whatever job they could find; many skimped along with the help of the federal College Students Employment Project. A few top students were supported by scholarships, most notably those recently endowed by Solon E. Summerfield. Mrs. Watkins' gift of a second women's cooperative hall was timely in 1937. Less timely and certainly less representative of the time are the young women dusting off a new Packard convertible.

In the mid-twenties President Coolidge posing with the Glee Club seems right. Has the President heard that economics professor John

Ise has been causing some stir throughout the state by teaching that Coolidge is a "tool in the hands of the big business interests"? Earlier chancellors had had to defend the University against charges of social elitism; Lindley had to defend the University against charges that the University harbored—even fostered—irreligious biologists, radical economists, subversive "red" students writing for the *Dove,* whose pink pages argued against militarism and for socialist programs. Even the *Kansan* (which had become a daily in 1912) by 1935 seemed to some small-town editors to have been taken over by "half-baked reds." The death of one student, Don Henry, while serving in the Abraham Lincoln Brigade in Spain, brought legislative investigation of the campus political climate. "Campus politics" and world politics drew closer together. One student managed briefly to hoist the red flag atop Fraser. Those returning for the fall semester after Hitler's invasion of Poland were still overwhelmingly isolationist and pacifist and opposed to American aid for Britain and France. But when the real war came, they went.

KU-MU game in new Memorial Stadium, 1921

The team with the uncrossed goal line

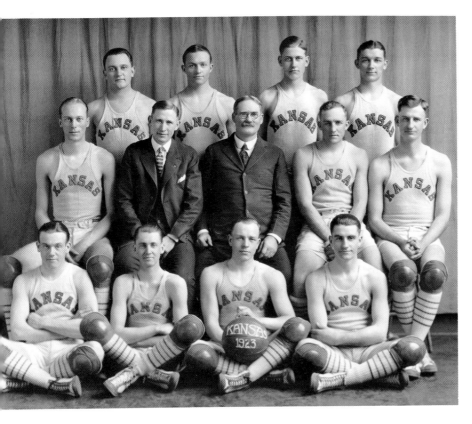

After seventeen years of Missouri Valley conference history, one basketball team has succeeded in winning a title without a single defeat and has played all conference opponents.

A five of superlative qualifications representing Kansas is the undefeated champion following a dramatic closing game against Missouri, when all doubt of Jayhawker court supremacy over the Tiger was banished. . . . The unprecedented basketball accomplishment of the Jayhawkers was made possible by five clean and capable young men working in full co-operation with Dr. Forrest C. Allen, athletic director and coach.

Graduate Magazine, March 1923

Undefeated basketball team   *Left to right, front row:* Armin Woestemeyer, Waldo Bowman, Paul Endacott, Andrew McDonald; *middle row:* John Wulf, Dr. F. C. Allen, Dr. James Naismith, Charlie Black, Byron Frederick; *back row:* Adolph Rupp, Bob Mosby, Tus Ackerman, Verne Wilkin

The Stadium? Yes! Unity of spirit among the members of an institution like a university is absolutely essential for the work the institution is to do. During the present period of unprecedented growth in universities this unity of spirit is more than ever necessary and more than ever difficult to secure. This unity must be achieved through an appeal to some human interests common to all the members of the institution. Athletics is one such interest. To be effective in accomplishing the above purpose, athletics must have modern facilities. The stadium is a most urgent necessity, not a luxury.

Dean F. J. Kelly, "The Kansas Stadium," September 1920

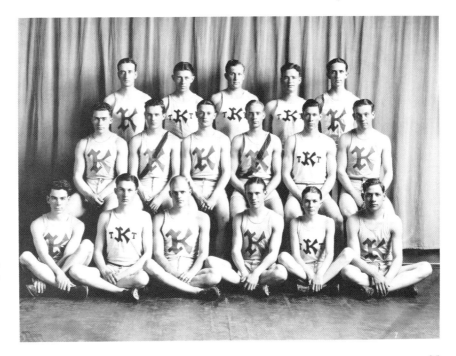

Track champions of the Missouri Valley Conference, 1923

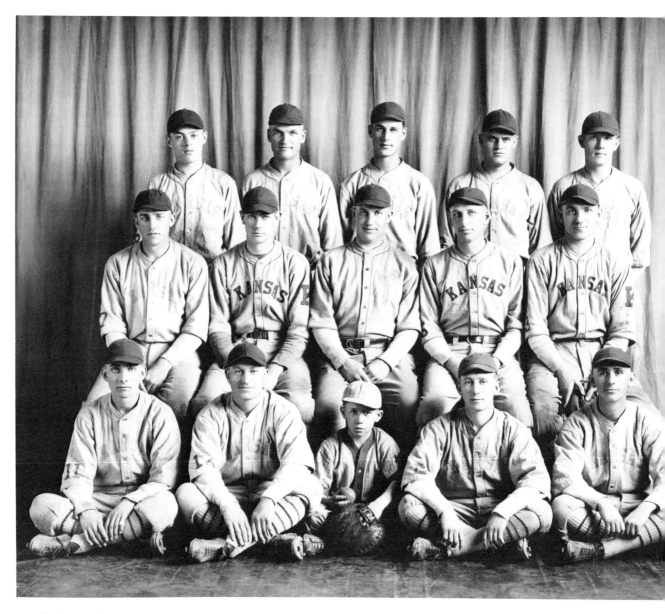

Conference champions, 1923

Not a few members of the Alumni Association can remember when there was no such thing as athletics for women. The most common form of athletic event for the gentler sex was the sewing circle; while the baking of cakes, pies, bread, etc., was thought to give all the exercise any woman would ever need.

But times have changed, and nowhere is the change more in evidence than in institutions of learning. The University of Kansas, which knew naught of women's athletics some years ago, now sponsors and encourages participation in sports by women. . . . K.U. women have their athletic association; and the best in each sport are awarded sweaters with letters, just as are the men.

Graduate Magazine, May 1924

KU team sets a world record in the Kansas Relays, 1925

Senior hockey team, 1926

Rifle Club, 1927

Hurdlers

1925

Fencers with Coach James Naismith, 1926

Potter Lake and the Acacia diving dog, 1914

99

Potter Lake isn't very big, but what a multitude of thrills it holds, given the proper proportions which are as follows: Twenty five percent damsels, twenty five percent males, twenty five percent water, twenty five percent swimming and diving. Mix well.

Jayhawker, 1927

1926

ROTC in the engineering parade, early 1920s

Bobsledding, 1928

Ice cream wagon on Jayhawk Boulevard, 1926

Fraser Hall

Professor and Mrs. Goldwin Goldsmith

Deserted Fraser is almost pathetic in its loneliness since the heart of the University has left it. . . . It was only yesterday that the work of administration went on in the rooms of the first floor of Fraser and students thronged the corridors all day long. . . . Though most of the students may be innocent of excess sentiment for old places and will forget Fraser and its former glories, the old building has yet a few friends who keep it in mind. Some of the men who have had offices in Fraser for many years frequently stop in to ''see how the remodeling is coming on'' they explain, but somehow one has a suspicion that they come because they like the old place. The new offices are much better, of course—more modern and everything, but the old building is home.

University Daily Kansan, January 25, 1924

In the heart of every alumnus of old K.U. is the sentiment that the memory of Uncle Jimmie Green may never die. To perpetuate it we must erect on the campus near Green Hall a memorial that will not only symbolize but idealize his life. To this end the James Woods Green Memorial Association has been organized. . . . We have selected Daniel Chester French, who, in the art of portraying personality, is the foremost sculptor of the world today.

Terrence J. Madden, in the *Graduate Magazine,* December, 1920

Dedication of Green memorial statue, 1926   Chancellor Lindley is fourth from left

Glee Club with President Coolidge in Washington, 1926

Ray Nichols

The K.U. Men's Glee Club performed well a mission of representing Kansas and the Missouri Valley Glee Club Association in the National Intercollegiate Glee Club Contest in New York March 6. It placed third in the contest and . . . the members of the organization so conducted themselves enroute to and from the contest at the places where they stopped that they earned many compliments for the University and themselves. The club was entertained at Schenectady, N.Y. by the alumni association there, and it spent a day in Washington, D. C. where it was presented to the President. . . . Kansas was the farthest west club ever to have sung in the national contest and was accorded considerable attention due to that fact.

Graduate Magazine, March 1926

The committee this year on the annual award to the ''Man whose influence had been most beneficial to the student body'' chose Raymond Nichols, '26, of Larned. . . . The choice seems to have struck a responsive chord in the student body for there seems to be general agreement that Nichols deserved the honor without question.

Nichols took his A.B. in 1926 and will receive his A.M. this year. He was editor of the Jayhawker in 1925, served on the Kansan Board and as editor of the student paper in 1925, was on the Dean's honor roll three years and is a Phi Beta Kappa, was Chief Sachem in 1926, member of Sigma Delta Chi, served as chairman of the Student County Club Committee 1926-27 and was elected president of the Men's Student Council last spring.

Graduate Magazine, May 1928

Watson Library, opened in 1924

Carrie Watson watching over the reading room

Dedication of Hoch, 1927

The Lawrence Choral Union with 450 voices, a children's chorus of 250 voices, the Minneapolis Symphony Orchestra comprising 60 pieces, and four noted soloists presented our own Prof. Chas. S. Skilton's oratorio "The Guardian Angel" May 2 in the new University Auditorium. The audience was thrilled with the immensity and beauty of the singing. It was the greatest musical body and perhaps the most important musical event ever held at the University.

Graduate Magazine, May 1928

Hoch Auditorium

Music week chorus and orchestra, 1928

Main gallery of the art museum

A collection of interest to art lovers and curio hunters is now very beautifully displayed [in the Spooner-Thayer Art Museum] at the University of Kansas in Lawrence. The exhibit is known as the W. B. Thayer memorial collection and was deeded to the university by Mrs. Thayer in 1917. . . . The building in which it is housed was formerly the university library but has been successfully adapted to the needs of a museum. The articles are arranged in cases made in the shops on the University campus. The estimated value of the collection is a quarter of a million dollars.

Margaret Whittemore, *American Magazine of Art,* June 1927

Chancellor Lindley speaking at Kansas Memorial Union groundbreaking ceremony, 1926

Kansas Memorial Union, opened in 1927

Memorial Union parade in front of Haworth Hall

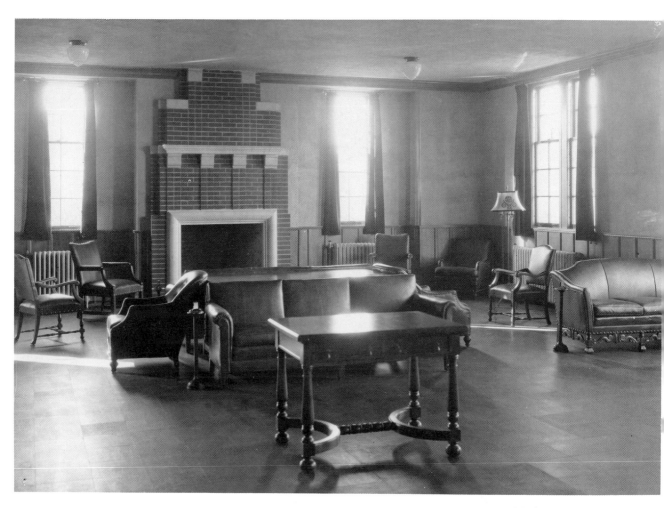

Men's lounge in the Union

LATE AFTERNOON RETREAT

In the lounge and in the brows-
    ing room,
They browse and lounge. The
    ineluctible doom
Of thought has wearied them.
    Their legs
Are flexible, twisted and doubled
    like pegs
Of taffy, wrapped in woolen
    socks and sneakers.
All day, in dingy classrooms,
    these young seekers
After knowledge have welcomed
    every potent word
With drowsy young indifference,
    having heard
Authority claim that knowledge
    comes unsought,

Union ballroom

Even if wisdom lingers and they
     remain untaught.
The only sound that breaks the
     cosy quiet
Of the hour comes as a soft and
     tuneful riot
Pervading with metallic tinkle the
     dusky space.
Balanced between the windows,
     the stern face
of T. S. Eliot, in pockmarked
     bronze, looks
Down its nose, and recommends
     that books
Be read, rather than idly used as
     props
For weary ankles when the brain-
     work stops.

   Helen Rhoda Hoopes, in a letter to
Katherine Kelley, August 28, 1961; University
Archives

Old Snow Hall, razed in 1934

Second Generation Club, 1928

112

Throughout America the decade just closing has been a period of unprecedented expansion in higher education. Colleges and universities have been almost swamped by numbers. Increased enrollment required additional building, equipment and personnel. Kansas has shared in this expansion. In proportion to population, Kansas has made a creditable showing in enrollment and in the effort to provide adequate facilities.

1930

New Snow Hall, opened in 1930

Space permits but bare enumeration of some of the chief events of the decade. Aside from the building program there are (1) the Memorial Campaign—which secured pledges of almost a million dollars for the Stadium, Green Memorial and Memorial Union; (2) Regents Law approved as providing for efficient control while insuring a large measure of academic freedom; (3) large gifts (a) Watkins Hall, and Henley Hall, (b) Beyland bequest for medical research, (c) Summerfield Scholarships insuring as many as forty men a full college course without financial anxiety, (d) many scholarships and other gifts; (4) establishment of the School of Business; (5) Dedication of Thayer Art Museum; (6) advance in scholastic standards; (7) evidence of increasing good will of people of the state toward the University; (8) admirable cooperation of faculty, students, alumni and the people of Lawrence in the effort to make the University more and more worthy of a great commonwealth.

Chancellor E. H. Lindley, in the *Graduate Magazine*, March 1930

Journalism faculty, 1930 *Left to right:* J. J. Kistler, Leon N. Flint, William A. Dill, Alfred Graves, William O. Harley, and Helen O. Mahin

Kansan office, 1935

1932 Olympic team *Left to right:* Glenn Cunningham, ''Buster'' Charles (Haskell), Coach Brutus Hamilton, Jim Bausch, and Clyde Coffman

Glenn Cunningham

Tau Sigma Dance Society, 1932

Kansas wheat was selling for 65 cents a bushel in the late summer of 1932, and the country was in the grip of the Great Depression.

Hoover said things were getting better. Roosevelt said they were getting worse. The November election would end the argument, but not the collapse of the economy. Meanwhile, an estimated 12 million people in the United States were "unemployed," the newly fashionable word for "out of work." . . .

With no prospect of a job, I came back to KU that September, after an absence of three years, sporting a white linen suit I had bought secondhand for $2 and hoping for a warm fall. There was little else in my wardrobe. I had $60, saved working on a seven-days-a-week summertime job at Fairyland Park in Kansas City, and a battered old Underwood I counted on to help me survive by typing themes and term papers for other students.

James Patterson, *Kansas Alumni,* June 1982

Hobo Day, 1934

Owl Society, 1935

Freshman induction, 1937

New students of the University stood and repeated a modified form of the old Athenian civic oath at the fourth annual new students initiation ceremonies September 29. It is here given: "We will never bring discredit to our University; we will cherish the ideals and sacred things of the University, both alone and with many; we will revere and obey the University's laws and do our best to incite a like respect and reverence in those about us; we will strive unceasingly to quicken the sense of civic duty and thus, in all these ways, we will strive to transmit this, our beloved University, not only, not less, but greater, better and more beautiful than it was transmitted to us."

Graduate Magazine, November 1927

Delta Tau Delta party, 1938

Chi Omegas polish a Packard

Women's Student Governance Association, mid 1930s

Mathematics Club *Front row:* U. G. Mitchell, third from
left; Wealthy Babcock, sixth; Gib Ulmer, Florence Black, and
Guy Smith

Henry Werner, Clyde Tombaugh, and Olin Templin

The death of Mrs. Elizabeth Miller Watkins brought to the University its greatest bequest and continued the generous and wise giving which she has been doing through the past thirteen years.

Having previously given to the University Watkins Hall, dormitory for self-supporting girls, in 1926, at a cost of $75,000; Watkins Memorial Student Hospital in 1931, at a cost of $190,000; Miller Hall, a second dormitory for self-supporting women, in 1936, at a cost of $75,000; and Watkins Nurses' Home in 1938, at a cost of $41,000, in her will she endowed Watkins and Miller Halls with a fund of $25,000 and the Student Hospital with a fund of $175,000. . . . The will furthermore provided that the Watkins home at the southeast corner of the campus should go to the University as the home of the Chancellor. . . . In addition she left to the Endowment Association of the University all her Kansas land outside of Douglas County.

Graduate Magazine, June 1939

Watkins Memorial Hospital, dedicated in 1931

Watkins and Miller Halls

Chancellor's residence

Elizabeth M. Watkins

Chancellor and Mrs. Lindley's reception, 1937

Everyone knows that the nineteen years of Chancellor Lindley's administration at the University of Kansas have been years of phenomenal growth, both physically and mentally. Chancellor Lindley came to the University at a time when war activities had for years denied the University the money it needed to build its physical plant. Now again, the new Chancellor will be confronted with the same problem in lesser degree because the building of the past has been sound. But he will have the problem nevertheless because for the past ten years while the needs of education have grown by leaps and bounds the legislatures have not found it possible to appropriate the funds which the University should have had. No plant can lie idle ten years and not need a lot of expense for betterment, so the new Chancellor will likely be called upon to choose wisely how he wishes to expend the money he can wrest from a reluctant legislature.

Two decades ago the great need was buildings. The University got them only to find that when it got ready to intensify its operative work the depression forestalled this and enforced rigid retrenchment. One of the lamentable features of the University is the small salaries that are being paid to faculty members. It is a wonder that Chancellor Lindley has retained as many good professors with other states bidding higher salaries for our best. Today the need for buildings is not as great as two decades ago, but the need to attract and encourage good professor talent is greater than ever. On this may depend the future usefulness of the University and it is hoped that the new Chancellor will lay his emphasis first on getting the educational quality of his instructors on a basis that will continue to give Kansas a University worthy of the name.

McPherson Republican, quoted in the *Graduate Magazine,* January 1939

Chancellor Lindley and Chancellor Malott, 1939

CHAPTER FIVE

War and Transition

BEGINNING WITH WORLD WAR II and continuing to the present, photographs of the University exist in plenitude and contain enormous amounts of data. Through memory and in their own way, many "readers" will give varied shapes to these more recent years evoked by the selected images. Even those who did not know the Hill during the forties will recognize the public pattern for that decade: waiting for war, war, the exuberant chaos that followed. This section opens with the volume's first night scene of the campus, but like the rest of the nation, the University would observe civil defense blackout drills. Soon lights came on earlier in the morning and stayed on later at night. Lights, like those in Fowler, with its round-the-clock technical training, Professor Taft recalls, made it "a weird sight on leaving the campus well past midnight to see the eerie glow of florescent lamps light all the windows of the Shops." New Chancellor Malott, an Abilene native, looks as confident, efficient, and idealistic as Eisenhower. Students digging dandelions and putting them in a Rinso box on a sunny spring day or those demonstrating for a day off after a win over Kansas State, just weeks before Pearl Harbor, may seem innocent and naïve; but, then, cameras are not particularly good at registering pervasive anxiety. Dean Paul Lawson helped dig the dandelions, but he was also publicly urging students to prepare to defend "the blessings of democracy and freedom" in the inevitable war. Lindley

Hall, under construction in 1941, would not become an academic building until 1946. For the duration, this first new structure since the twenties became an army barracks and mess. Navy machinists barracked in Strong, displacing among others John Ise, who was not heard to grumble. The machinists and later electricians marched to Fowler Shops for training, and then marched back to string their white laundry across the brow of the hill above the stadium where, in Taft's words, there was "physical training for everyone—except faculty." Big-time football bided its time, awaiting the postwar boom years.

Coeds talk with sailors on the steps of Marvin Hall in its full summer foliage: by 1943 only ten percent of the students were civilian men. Summer school, first begun in 1903, was expanded into a full third semester. Vacations were curtailed as the University went round-the-year as well as the clock to accommodate an array of military and war-related programs, including flight training, courses for women working in the Wichita aircraft industry, and basic chemistry for workers from the huge Sunflower munitions plant twelve miles east of town. Workers as well as students and navy men drank beer and danced outside at the Dine-a-Mite tavern south of town on Twenty-third Street. More than at any previous time the University became a microcosm of the community; the distinction between "town" and "gown" was permanently blurred. Instructors, workers, students, all lived in any space they could find in a small university town already short of housing after a decade-long depression. Housing problems could only get worse. Enrollment a month after the Japanese surrender in August 1945 was fairly orderly. But with demobilization and the G.I. Bill in force, nearly twice as many students as had ever been on the Hill enrolled for the fall of 1946. Town attics and basements took some of the overflow. The military barracks in Lindley and Strong were needed for classrooms, but single men could bunk under the stadium; some displaced Mrs. Thayer's collection in Spooner Museum. Married students replaced munitions workers in the housing at Sunflower Ordnance Works and made the twenty-five-mile round trip to campus by bus until gasoline, tires, and cars became more plentiful. To the housing was soon added the parking problem. Cars crowded the campus, never to leave. What better way than washing cars to raise money for charity? or for oneself by selling parking space at the Missouri game?

New buildings were planned but not built during the late forties. Immensely increased funding, much of it now from the federal government, went for temporary barracks, for expansion of the library, for conversion of old buildings to peaceful academic pursuits, such as journalism moving into the shops where the machinists had trained. Clerical workers and maintenance personnel were needed, as was a large staff to help feed, house, and keep healthy 10,000 or so students. The wartime faculty's ranks were joined by hundreds of new professors and graduate assistants, who created their small city on the southern "Sunnyside" of the Hill in wooden barracks hauled in from closed military bases. Hordes of students' children on campus changed the image of a young, unattached "Joe College"; veterans and foreign students stimulated classes and pushed grade averages up; football players, matured and toughened by the war, went to the Orange Bowl. Government checks—though never enough at $90–$100 a month—made payday lively in Lawrence. Sunnyside apartments may look a bit like a rural ghetto, but the campus

Chancellor Deane W. Malott

proper became prettier than ever. The lilac hedge established east of Fraser before the turn of the century was now rivaled by an entire campus of crab apple, ornamental pear, forsythia; red tulips appeared in front of Hoch, pale yellow jonquils in front of Lindley. Only two permanent structures appeared in the years immediately after the war. Both were more symbolic than utilitarian. In 1946 Danforth Chapel was available for the wedding rites of students who married while still at KU; the married student became a commonplace member of the University family; the World War II Memorial Campanile was dedicated the same month the Selective Service gave its first tests for temporary deferment from service in the Korean War. That was May 1951. Chancellor Malott, Class of '21, had accepted the presidency of Cornell; Franklin Murphy, Class of '36, would take over in the fall.

128

With no disparagement to the leaders of the past, let it be said that under Deane Malott, K.U. really began to flower. Partly it was the times, partly it was the man. Guiding the University through the all-out World War II period was the greatest challenge the institution ever faced—through the war itself, with shrunken enrollments as the sons of K.U. fought on the far-flung global battlefields; in the after-war period, with the huge influx of returned G.I.s swamping the already expanded facilities as never before. . . . So the University emerged from this period of abnormality not weakened, but stronger than ever in quality of education, in plant equipment, and in the soul and spirit of the school.

    Roy Roberts, quoted in Fred Ellsworth, ''Our Amazing Chancellors,'' in *Alumni Magazine*

Students leaving convocation in Hoch Auditorium

Dandelion Day, 1941   Dean Paul B. Lawson is to the back

Pep rally, 1941

Students march to demand holiday after victory over K-State, 1941

Women's co-ops, 1942

Lindley Hall, dedicated in 1942

Navy training on campus, 1942

It is the fundamental duty of K.U. men and women to train themselves for maximum leadership, for maximum understanding, and for maximum service. To this end the entire resources of the University are pledged, that by our deeds and words we may help this nation to pass through the flames of war, and to emerge victorious and free. The University of Kansas has given distinguished service to our nation in two other wars. It will do so again.

Chancellor Deane Malott, quoted in the *Graduate Magazine,* 1942

Navy machinist mates training in Fowler Shops

A lot of us are unsettled in our own minds about just what to do. We're going to serve and do our part, whatever that takes. I don't hear anyone talking about actual combat or not coming back. We're thinking about our futures but that's something you can't plan for anymore.

KU student, quoted by Alvin McCoy, *Kansas City Star*, 1942

Mrs. Malott helps feed the troops

During the busiest hours [on the University telephone exchange] two operators are necessary to take care of the extra calls. Records show that about 2000 calls are handled daily and on some days this number is considerably larger.

Mrs. Mary Neustifter, chief operator, who has been plugging away at her post for 14 years, has become a tradition in the office. She is able to recognize the voices of all members of the faculty and prefers that the callers ask for the person rather than the number.

"Usually the number of calls falls during vacation periods," Mrs. Neustifter said, "but not this year—the war has changed that." The "Voice of Oread" estimates that she has said "KU" over 5,000,000 times.

Jayhawker, 1943

Mary Neustifter

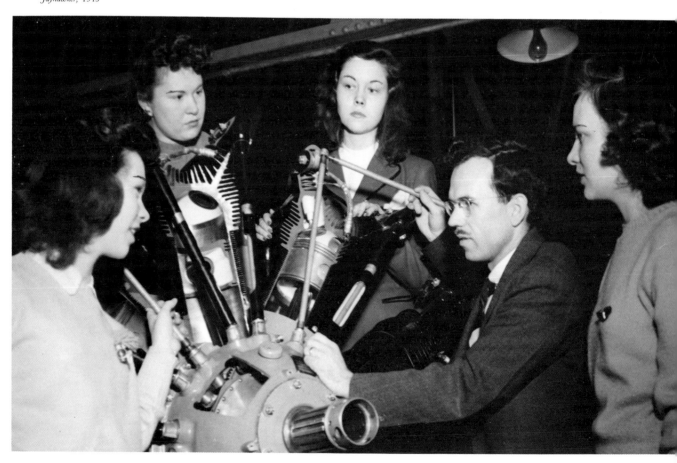

Aeronautical engineering

At the Dine-a-Mite, 1943

And then there were all the good college hangouts. The Union fountain with good cokes and Pi Phi's; the Cottage with cokes and sandwiches and Alpha Chi's; the "Mite" with good beer, a loud juke box, defense workers, and dancing on the patio; and the Pit where the boys gathered for evenings of male conversation and Budweiser. The unofficial night games in Memorial stadium were good, too.

Jayhawker, 1945

Laurence Woodruff, registrar and military coordinator

Helen Rhoda Hoopes, assistant professor of English

How was it at KU in the '40s during World War II?
. . . It was a time of spirit, dedication and
commitment, of solidarity and purpose. It was one
of those worst-of-times that brings forth the best in
people and in institutions. . . . All of it was a feast
for me—the books everywhere, the conversations,
the beauty of the campus. . . . There was help and
encouragement on every hand: Marie Miller step-
ping out of the Dean of Women's office in old
Fraser, catching me on my way to work to tell me of
a place to live, a scholarship, a job; Mr. [Harold]
Ingham apprenticing me to edit the extension
newsletter; Raymond Nichols and Laurence Woodruff and Fred Ellsworth advising me like kind uncles;
Mildred Seaman, KFKU director, introducing me to
classical music. . . . In the lecture rooms and labs
and libraries, I found the true ambrosia. Work, off
and on campus, and organizational life and dorm life
were great, but the main show was always in a
classroom.

Bert Nash, professor of education

During the war, many faculty members stayed on
beyond retirement, or came back. They and other
seasoned faculty members taught introductory as
well as advanced classes. Underclassmen learned
from the folks who wrote the books: Leon ''Daddy''
Flint re-ran his legendary lectures; Helen Rhoda
Hoopes thundered away in the heights of Fraser,
daring one and all to learn and love literature and
language; L. L. Louden, handsome enough to be in
pictures, made geology jump with tales of his
adventures; Hilden Gibson soapboxed his way into
the consciousness of even the least political and most
reluctant; Professor Patterson, in a dark basement
room in Strong, pronounced ''Roman Empire'' with
a rolling rumble in a medieval history course; . . .
Martha Peterson taught me algebra, advised me and
put me under her wing; Ruth Hoover, to her
surprise and mine, passed me, C-worthy, in
swimming; and John Ise, ah! John Ise!, aroused a
liberal streak that will forever be part of me. . . .
My mentor was Elmer Beth, who goaded and guided
my career in journalism.

Delores Sulzman Hope, in *Kansas Alumni,* September 1982

What sort of problems does a professor face in
planning his life? . . . First, I decided early that I
wanted little or nothing to do with local affairs—
except to sing in choirs. I was a servant of the State,
not of Lawrence, and my duty was to the people of
Kansas.

Second, I decided rather soon that I would spend
the least time possible on committees, because they
bored me and they seldom had anything worth-while

John Ise, professor of economics

to do. There are professors who spend many hours every week on committees, and I honor them for it, but I find such work debilitating and unprofitable. Someone has said ''a committee is a group of the unfit, chosen by the unwilling, to do the unnecessary.''

Third, I always wished that I could become better acquainted with more of my students. I developed a real respect for students—at any rate for KU students—and always had a feeling that they were worthy of better than I could give them. . . .

Fourth, I always wished I could read more, study more, learn more about economics than I did. I envied professors who could read widely and remember what they read; but my memory was only fair, and so I decided to write books for others to read instead of devoting my time largely to reading other men's books. I am not sure that this was wise, but it is too late to think about it now. . . .

I was never satisfied with my plan of life. I always wanted to do more of everything, and yet slighted everything, in spite of very hard work. I seldom took off week-ends or vacation periods for recreation. Perhaps in my next reincarnation I can do better.

John Ise, in the *Jayhawker,* 1962

Enrollment, 1945

Jayhawk Boulevard

Actives and pledges both are to report all grades to Penny after each test. Song practices for pledges are to be held Thurs. evening before dinner. Housebills are to be presented in an itemized account the first and are due by the tenth of each month. Actives and pledges are to be seated alternately at dinner. Pictures will be taken of the house Thurs. at 5:30. Girls will wear pastel slip-over sweaters with single strand pearls and dark skirts.

Delta Gamma *Record,* October 4, 1943

Kappa Kappa Gamma

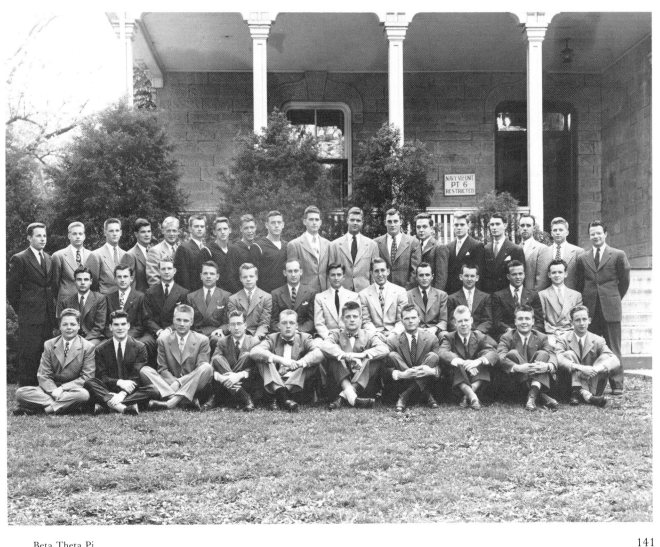

Veterans protest housing, 1946

Allen Crafton auctions faculty services for World Student
Service Fund, 1945

Sunflower Village

The Jayhawk family is no longer nestled atop and on the brow of the Hill. It has spread to all suburbs of Lawrence, and a number of students find themselves commuting via the Rapid Transit.

Student renters started out with "choosey" ideas. Many of them wanted the companionship offered by organized houses— that being out of the question, they thought they could do with a nice, spacious room—something with all the comforts of home, modern facilities, thick rugs, ample closets, and a beauty-rest mattress. At the end of several days' search some were ready to settle for a closet with a pull-down mattress and a priority on the bathtub every other Saturday.

Jayhawker, 1945

The housing problem is most serious for married students, particularly those with children, and for negro students. Married students will be riding that bus from Sunflower Village for several semesters. Married students find that those "little bundles of joy" complicate the housing problem considerably and complete the the farce of attempting to "subsist" on $90 a month of subsistence pay.

To remain within the bounds of accepted language, the best thing to say about negro housing is nothing. As in so many other matters, the negro's lot in housing is not a good one, and adds weight to the contention that "equal rights" for the negro is seldom found outside the Constitution. Finding a place to eat is also a problem for the negro student, since the only accessible source of meals for negroes in Lawrence is the Union cafeteria. Privately operated restaurants re-

Dean Paul Lawson and Chancellor Malott wash cars for World Student Service Fund

143

fused to serve food to negroes, although local officials cheerfully drafted them as ''equals'' into the armed forces. The unavoidable conclusion is ''You were good enough to fight for me, but not to eat with me.''

Jayhawker, 1946

Sunnyside, oh Sunnyside,
How we love thee Sunnyside,
We love thy floors' unvarnished light,
Love thy doors that fit so tight.
We may scoff, complaints be free,
But without thy roof,
Where would we be?
Eudora, Baldwin or K.C.

Jayhawker, 1962

Danforth Chapel, dedicated in 1946

Sunnyside housing development

A Danforth wedding

Last stand of freshman beanies, 1947

KU-MU game, 1947

Ray Evans

Orange Bowl, 1948

Football, 1947 *Left to right:* Don Fambrough; Vic Bradford, backfield coach; Bob Ingalls, line coach; Otto Schnellbacker

Endowment Association trustees, 1949 *Left to right, seated:*
Irving Hill, Fred M. Harris, Irvin Youngberg, Mrs. Flora
Boynton, Mrs. Will T. Beck, C. C. Stewart; *standing:* Justice
Walter G. Thiele, John H. Kane, Oscar S. Stauffer, Dean
Paul B. Lawson, Frank C. Carson, George E. Nettels,
Maurice L. Breidenthal, Byron Shutz, August W. Lauterbach,
Riley Burcham, Chancellor Deane W. Malott, Senator Will
T. Beck, Dean Franklin Murphy

Twenty-fifth reunion of the undefeated Missouri Valley
League basketball champions of 1923 *Left to right, back
row:* John P. Wulf, Armin Woestemeyer, Dr. F. C. "Phog"
Allen, Tusten Ackerman, Paul Endacott, Adolph Rupp, Charles
Black, Verne Wilkin, Waldo Bowman, J. Robert Mosby, Byron
C. Frederick; *front row:* Dan Statton, Andrew McDonald,
George V. Glaskin, Ward Hitt, William Crosswhite

Templin Scholarship Hall

Ten campus queens, 1949

Deane Malott, aided by Mrs. Malott, made another particularly felicitous contribution to the University. That was beautification of the campus. If Chancellor Marvin, back in the '70s, was a pioneer in planting the campus, then Malott was a latter-day master in revamping and rejuvenating the face of Mt. Oread.

The interim chancellors each contributed. Dr. Lindley had the help of the incomparable Belgian gardener, Van Horbeck. It was he who made grass and shrubs grow on the rocky plot east of Fraser Hall. He planted the rows of elms which now shade Jayhawk Boulevard, the main campus traffic artery.

But when Chancellor Malott arrived after the droughts of the '30s, he employed a landscape architect and started a revamping campaign of major proportions. The south side of the Hill was rounded off and revamped around the new buildings there, the Military Science building and the site of Malott Hall-to-be. The north side of the Hill had the World War II Memorial Drive and Campanile. The Class of '45 planted 1,200 flowering crab trees around the north brow—and Mrs. Malott went personally and watered them to be sure they grew.

Shrubs and trees were transplanted. Sidewalks were relocated. Groups of shrubs which the campus population had thought attractive in 1939, before the Malotts arrived, were cleaned out and trimmed vigorously. It was a pleasing transformation.

Fred Ellsworth, "Our Amazing Chancellors: War and Aftermath," *Alumni Magazine*

Sarge in spring

Lilac Lane

Campus beautification

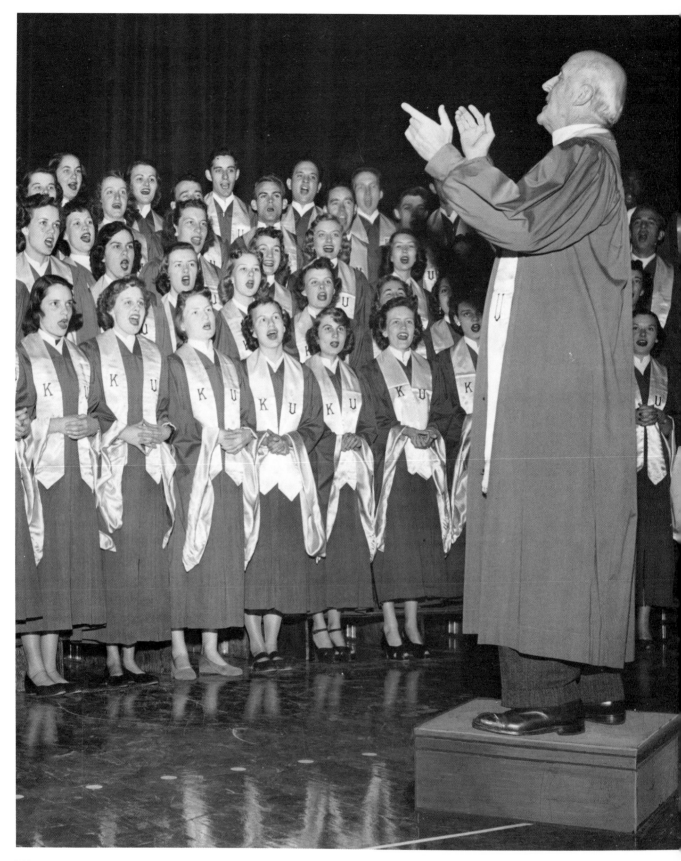

The Concert Choir, directed by Dean Donald M. Swarthout

CHAPTER SIX

Prosperity

THE PROSPEROUS FIFTIES open with the composer Virgil Thompson praising the University and its music, choral and orchestral, as well as a retrospective twenties' song-and-dance and the ringing of the memorial bells. A young, energetic, forceful Franklin Murphy became chancellor in time to see Dr. ''Phog'' Allen's basketball team beat not only big-city St. John's for the national title but the Russians at the Helsinki Olympics. Big centers Lovellette and Born were succeeded by Wilt Chamberlain, who opened in the new Fieldhouse with a dunk-shot against astonished, flat-footed Northwestern. And there were world-class weightmen and milers. The University was anxious to be in the national and international arena. The United Nations police action in Korea affected many individual students, but it did not disrupt life on the Hill the way earlier wars had. Students came to the campus from most of the ''free world''; study abroad had become relatively common for Kansas students. The term nationally known, or even internationally known, was attached more frequently to the names of scholars: Raymond Hall in zoology; Charles Michener in entomology; Charlton Hinman, who adapted World War II bomb-sight techniques to the study of Shakespeare's texts. Monies from the federal government, from industry, from prospering alumni, supported research as diverse as therapy by music or planning a city. Pushed by Graduate Dean John Nelson and by Raymond Nichols in 1951,

Malott asked the state legislature for funds not just for instruction and building but for scholarly research. Murphy kept asking for—and often getting—more for the state's General Research Fund to encourage a young and growing faculty to discover and create new knowledge, not just to transmit the old. Honors programs pushed undergraduates towards Rhodes, Woodrow Wilson, Marshall, and Fulbright scholarships. The library acquired special collections in science, economics, history, and literature. With the veterans' temporary bunks gone, Spooner was reorganized into a proper Museum of Art, opening on February 1, 1951. Acquisition of a collection began in earnest. Vestiges of the war are few in these photographs: some barracks remain, and Hazel Anderson uses an ammunition box to sort books in the Law Library. A peaceful, scholarly seriousness pervades many of the photos of classrooms and laboratories. Even the new theater's costume workshop and make-up room seem quietly professional. There may be a card game or two going on in the Hawk's Nest, but most are there on a mid-morning ''study-break,'' perhaps to discuss what to enroll in now that required biology and speech classes have already filled up. Some, no doubt, argue with animation about the McCarthy hearings, the Chinese army's entry into Korea or the Soviet's into Hungary.

Functional, no-nonsense, efficient buildings rose on the edges of the Hill. Two buildings had been completed during the war. The Military Science Building (1943) begun by the WPA had some castle-like forms and a steep-pitched red roof in keeping with the older campus; Lindley (1942) was more severely geometrical and had a flat roof useful for water tanks, elevator heads, or later, air-conditioning units. It was the progenitor of buildings to come. The first was Malott Hall, designed from the inside out for the needs of the physical sciences; ''the resulting outside appearance,'' Business Manager J. J. Wilson announced rather defiantly, ''will be a minor point.'' The same might have been said of Allen Field House or the new homes for the Business and Engineering Schools, Summerfield and Learned. Music and theater, which had been shunted about the campus for a century, got a building more pleasing and varied in shape and texture. It appropriately took the name of the chancellor who was both promoter and patron of the arts—Murphy. The aerial view for 1955 was taken from the southwest, the direction the University was growing. In the far northeastern corner, a complex of women's dorms—closing hours rigidly enforced—has filled up Old North College hill. Behind the camera, the Daisy Field awaits married students' apartments and the coed dorms that began to go up in 1958. Out of

sight to the right, below the flags of Fraser, a small campus of scholarship halls for bright but needy students has grown up. Battenfeld, Sellards, Pearson, Stephenson, Douthart, Grace Pearson Halls, lend some Georgian grace to a neighborhood of rented rooms quickly slipping downhill. At the far western end of the boulevard, a fountain copied from the garden of an eighteenth-century Northumberland manor house splashes on an early spring day.

The sixties were not just a time of tearing down, but there was a lot of it. Old buildings went. First Blake, then, dramatically and more photogenically, the towers of Fraser were gone. Both buildings were replaced on their sites with structures vaguely reminiscent of the originals. When Robinson Gym and Haworth came under the wrecking ball, their namesakes migrated down the southern slope and assumed the prevailing style of boxy containers. Still, all would agree that the new natatorium improves upon the Styx-like pool in the bowels of the old gym. Where that pool had been, there lay for too long a large hole where Chancellor Wescoe wanted a great building to bring the humanities—philosophy, languages, history, literature—back to the center of the University. Inflation and budget restraints—not student protests—delayed the building of Wescoe Hall;

but students took a lot of the chancellor's time. From the civil rights movement they had learned the method of patient waiting to enforce their just and clearly stated demand that racial barriers be torn down. Protest stayed peaceful for awhile. On April 22, 1967, around Potter's pond, colorfully if bizarrely dressed students celebrated humanity against war at a "Human Be-In." It featured not only penny gum but a wild bunch of East and West Coast poets who, to the puzzlement of local hippies, abandoned the festivities for the Kansas Relays to see Jim Ryun try to shatter his old world record. Around the Union and north past the Gaslight Tavern and down to the old Rock Chalk cafe, something called "street life" as opposed to "student life" was evolving. Hair got longer, feet barer, music louder, voices more strident and angry.

Rock Chalk Revue, 1951

At the University of Kansas, in Lawrence, all the music techniques are practiced with expertness by a large student body and a faculty of over fifty. . . . Several of the student works in large form seemed to [your correspondent] in every way the equal of the best professional work by young composers that we hear in Tanglewood, at the Composers' Forum and in the downtown New York concerts. And it was ever so delightful to observe how a great seriousness pervades it all, a deep and tender poetry as of the Kansas Plains, a sweetness and a nobility of thought that are rarer in the Seaboard cities than one might wish. The University of Kansas, of course, has been a major musical center for half a century. Its high standards and general effectiveness are not a mushroom growth.

Virgil Thompson, in the *New York Sun;* reprinted in *Alumni Magazine,* March 1951

Installation of memorial bells

The K. U. World War II Memorial is in use. The bells of the carillon ring out over the campus and across the valley on regular schedules. A constant stream of cars rolls along memorial driveway. . . .

The dedication ceremonies May 27 brought a crowd of 7,000 persons. . . .

Wonderment pervaded the crowd sitting in the north bowl of the stadium and scattered over the hillside for three quarters of a mile, as Anton Brees, guest carillonneur, opened with "America" and proceeded on through "Crimson and The Blue," "Lead Kindly Light" and other hymns and folk tunes. The audience was delighted. It was a music new to Kansas.

Alumni Magazine, June 1951

World War II Memorial Campanile, 1951

It has occurred to me that if the University memorial to the men who served in the war should take the form of a Community House, there would be no further need of reserving Fowler Shops for use as University Commons. In that case the Department of Journalism wishes to make formal request that the possibility of using that building for printing, Journalism and University publications generally be considered.

Letter from Professor Leon N. Flint to Chancellor Strong, April 1919; Flint Correspondence, University Archives

Flint Hall, 1952

Nightshirt parade, 1951 *Left to right:* Chancellor Franklin D. Murphy, student Jim Logan, and Dean Lawrence C. Woodruff

Viewing championship game on TV in Kansas Memorial Union, 1952

NCAA championship team, 1952

What happened to the K. U. team?

The gang who had seemed potentially great for three years turned a corner. It was along about the middle of February that the boys rose to swamp Oklahoma A & M—and then Missouri—then Kansas State—Oklahoma—and Colorado to become Big Seven champions. . . . After the Big Seven race the Jayhawkers mowed down TCU 68 to 64 and St. Louis U. 74-55 in the NCAA regional. . . . In Seattle in the NCAA finals they sidetracked Santa Clara 74 to 55 and St. John's 80 to 63. Then . . . Phog Allen's '52 crew defeated Southwestern State Teachers, NAIB winners, 92 to 65, for the right to play in New York City for the National Collegiate Championship. . . . Two nights later they defeated LaSalle College of Philadelphia 70 to 65. That victory put the Kansas team automatically on the American Olympic squad in Helsinki in late July. . . . Clyde Lovellette, heralded as among the greatest cagers of all time, smashed every record of the NCAA while in Seattle. . . . Vincent O'Keefe of the Seattle Times put it this way. "You went out to the Pavilion without any love for the guy. . . . But before the game was over you were standing up and cheering Clyde Lovellette on to greater scoring feats. You watched the broad, homely face crease in a big smile as he accepted the congratulations of the opposing coach and you went away from the Pavilion thinking nothing but good of ol' "Humphrey Pennyworth."

Jayhawker, March 1952

Waiting for the team

Left to right: Mrs. Franklin D. Murphy, Chancellor Murphy, and Coach Phog Allen

Hawk's Nest, Kansas Memorial Union, 1950s

Basketball in Hoch Auditorium, 1953

Kansas Memorial Union   Frank Burge, director of Kansas Memorial Union, at right in group around piano

Campus Chest Drive dance, 1953

What you call teaching is just half of education. The other half is learning. Students don't do all the learning around here. In any proper university the faculty are learning. Most of this learning, at least on the frontiers, is what we call research.

William J. Argersinger, Jr., associate dean of the Graduate School, *Alumni Magazine,* October 1962

E. Raymond Hall, professor of zoology

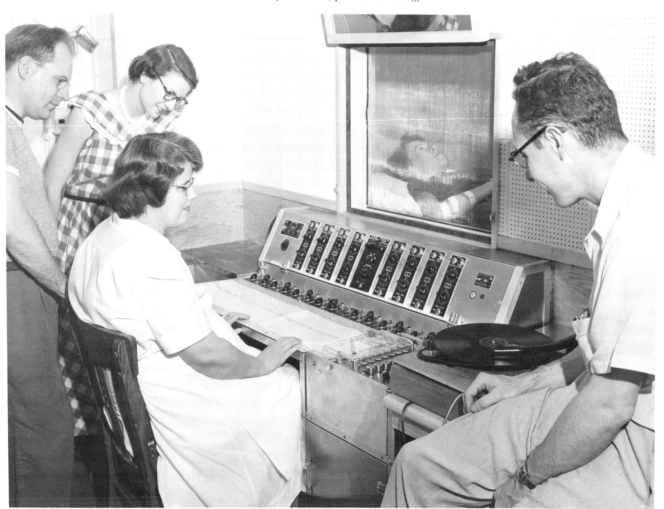

Music therapy, 1953   Virginia Detlor is at the console

Charles D. Michener, professor of entomology

Governmental Research Center, 1953   Professor Ethan Allen, director, second from right

1954

During the next fifty years, more than 27,000 engineers, doctors and pharmacists of the future will be graduated from the University of Kansas. For all of them, chemistry will serve as a basic science—a cornerstone upon which their professional life will be built. . . . Modern research is intricate and complex. The days when startling discoveries are made with only a beaker and a stirring rod are unfortunately past. A top-notch teaching and research staff can be attracted and held only if modern facilities for research are available. Until Science [Malott] Hall came into being, that was the one factor that threatened the excellence of the teaching and research programs at the University of Kansas. . . . Thanks to Science Hall, the University of Kansas has begun a "Chemical Revolution" . . . that will serve the state and help to spark its economy for many years to come.

Ray Q. Brewster, chairman, chemistry department, *Alumni Magazine,* October 1954

Architecture students

Chi Omega Fountain dedication, 1955

Oregon Trail Marker dedication, 1954 *Left to right:* Professor Robert Taft, Chancellor Franklin D. Murphy, Howard Driggs, Dean Wood, Professor George Anderson, Mrs. Driggs, and librarian Robert Vosper

Pharmacy class

[Each] new college program recalls the uproar caused by changes in past years. . . . The ''group'' systems still in use under a modified version was first instituted in 1909. The imposition of the English proficiency examination was first applied to those who received degrees in 1940. The examination in Western Civilization and the biology requirement were added in 1945 after ''heated and wordy'' battles at faculty meetings.

None of these . . . could hold a candle to the requirements in the early days. Before 1880 a student didn't have to worry about filling requirements—there would have been no choice since there were no electives. It is certain he wouldn't have had a foreign language deficiency. He took six semesters of Greek and five of Latin before the senior year.

And maybe today's student wouldn't have been able to get by the placement exams of 1899. Typical questions were: ''Name five of the most noted Colonial governors, and write a brief sketch of the work of each,'' ''Give the causes and results of the great revolutions that have taken place since the year 1600,'' and ''Give the laws of electro-magnetic induction, and describe the induction coil, the magneto and the dynamo.''

Alumni Magazine, May 1959

In the fall of 1955, the university announced a program designed especially for the ''gifted student.'' Its objective: to make sure that exceptional young men and women would not be overlooked or under-exposed in a time of great student population and limited faculty. . . . When they arrive at the university as freshmen, [selected] students find themselves in touch with a special faculty committee. It has the power to waive many academic rules for them. They are allowed to take as large a bite of education as they can swallow, and the usual course prerequisites do not apply; they may enter junior and senior-level courses if they can handle the work. They use the library with the same status as faculty members and graduate students, and some serve as short-term research associates for professors. The force of the program has been felt beyond the students and faculty members who are immediately involved. It has sent a current throughout the College of Liberal Arts and Sciences. . . . The value of the program reaches down into the high schools, too, stimulating teachers and attracting to the university strong students who might otherwise be lost to Kansas.

''Special Report on American Higher Education,'' 1958; reprinted in *Alumni Magazine,* March 1958

The big board—enrollment, 1955

Undergraduate honors program, 1956   Professor Francis Heller at left, Dean George W. Waggoner at extreme right

General Psychology I, 1958   Professor Herbert F. Wright, with back to camera

Law School librarian Hazel Anderson

Mock United Nations

Foreign students in Professor E. E. Bayles' class

Pinning

Wilt Chamberlain

Allen Field House, 1956

Track stars Bill Nieder, Les Bitner, and Al Oerter, 1956

Murphy Hall, 1957

Costume room, Murphy Hall

Commencement dinner, 1957 *Left to right:* Piano Professor Jan Chiapusso, Gertrude Sellards Pearson, and Distinguished Service citee Edward F. Kohman

Learning make-up techniques, Murphy Hall

Summerfield Hall, 1959

Steps from Memorial Drive to Bailey

Skiing down Mount Oread

175

Billy Mills

Learned Hall

Daisy Field dorms going up

1959 NCAA championship track squad   Track coach Bill Easton, far left, second row

I have shared the pride of the state and the area in what I believe has been modest progress at the University during these years, progress achieved in spite of unreasonable and indeed unprecedented handicaps. It is especially hard to contemplate leaving the faculty and staff of the University, those members of the legislature, and those enlightened Kansans in all parts of the State who have so believed in the future of Kansas and its children that they have been willing to work through these last years, often against great odds, to ensure the continued development of the University. . . . I shall always be in their debt.

Chancellor Franklin D. Murphy, resignation statement, March 1960, in *University Daily Kansan*

Homecoming

Left to right: sports announcer Tom Hedrick and basketball
coach Dick Harp

KU goes abroad, 1961

It began with an American student's hospitable gesture. The friendly way in which he took it for granted that he should take us to our new homes in his car was the nicest possible welcome to us as foreign students. We soon discovered that this attitude was not merely zeal for the new, but a genuine desire to help. Frequent "hi's" and a smile from students unknown to you . . . the sincere interest . . . in your country and in how you do things there; all this helped so much to get quickly over the first hard days in a foreign country. . . . I am sure that every one of us has an undivided admiration for the beautiful campus of KU. There are no stern, forbidding houses built closely together, as is often the case in Europe, but buildings which give the impression of quiet and distinguished well-being. The dorms, with their modern and tasteful furniture and all the facilities you can think of, and hot water every

The world comes to KU, 1962

day, the big lounges with their soft, comfortable easy chairs and carpets, the theater and the stadium, are all luxuries that a foreign student, unused to on the campuses of Europe, will certainly take advantage of and enjoy with gratitude.

Irmgard Kinzig, in the *Jayhawker,* 1961

Museum of Art exhibition opening, 1962   Professor Marilyn Stokstad, center

Faculty and alumni plan HELP-KU (Higher Education Loan Program), 1961 *Left to right:* Cora M. Downs, Solon E. Summerfield Distinguished Professor of Bacteriology; Raymond C. Moore, Solon E. Summerfield Distinguished Professor of Geology; Ray Q. Brewster, professor of chemistry; Olin Petefish, and Dolph Simons, Jr.

Awards for scholarly writing *Left to right:* Charlton Hinman, professor of English; Chancellor W. Clarke. Wescoe; and Fritz Heider, professor of psychology

With so many new buildings completed on top of
Mount Oread since the teen years and the twenties,
with so many more students, so many more
automobiles, with the trees so much larger, the overall impression is that of greater activity and less
space. I can make this exception—the building to the
south and southwest where the land purchased by
the Endowment Association is being utilized to such
good advantage—does bring a realization of how
much bigger our University has become.
Alfred G. "Scoop" Hill, in the *Alumni Magazine,* February 1953

Razing Blake, 1963

Daisy Field, 1967

Hashinger Hall, a view from Pioneer Cemetery

Some persons contend that Fred Ellsworth dropped off the back of the Ark when it passed over Mt. Oread. Others say he simply showed up the day K.U. opened in 1866. But the truth of the matter is Fred has just begun his 30th year as secretary of the Alumni Association. . . . In the continuing growth and change and evolution of the University through booms, depressions, wars, and in all kinds of political and economic environments, there has remained that one constant factor that bound all together, giving them direction and purpose, not alone for the problems of the moment but for those of the distant future that so few men are able to envision.

That was Fred Ellsworth.

Alumni Magazine, February 1965

Fred Ellsworth

Spring fling

Business School enrollment   Professor Charles Saunders, second from right

Telephone Executives Course, Business School, 1963   Professor Frank Pinet, at center

New Blake Hall, 1964

Band Day, 1964

Gale Sayers

Left to right: Law student Al Hicks; his wife, education student Judith Hicks; and their children, Traci and Kevin

187

The university's concern must be with the search for truth and its perfection. . . . Primary to the university's search is discussion—free and open; discussion, I said, not demonstration. It is only discussion that allows for complete examination of all the facts and all their facets, that prevents the mechanization of the mind and the sterilization of the spirit. . . . All this you must have learned—and this as well—that everything must be considered as it exists, in a matrix, that knowledge's purpose is to understand all things in terms of interrelationships. That learning is the making of the educated man, one who recognizes that no simple question can be asked, no simple answer provided and no simple solution proposed. Lastly, I trust you have learned that discussion leads to progress—and that progress can best be made if situations are not polarized, if one group is not set against another, if we abandon the search for villains. In a university generations cannot be set against each other as they would be by some who claim that no one over thirty can be trusted. . . . Students, faculty, administration, alumni, are all part of one continuum. The university, created for change, is based on trust, trust that given a proper share of the nation's wealth, it will create change responsibly and make for a better society. Trust is a fragile instrument—it is the responsibility of all of us to maintain it.

Chancellor W. Clarke Wescoe, in his Farewell to the Graduates, June 1966; Wescoe Speeches, University Archives

Greek discrimination protest, 1964

Civil rights protest, 1965

Strong Hall sit-in, 1965

New Robinson Gymnasium, 1966

Fraser falls, 1965

Swim meet in Robinson Gymnasium

Chancellor Wescoe at basketball rally, 1966

Chancellors Murphy, Malott, and Wescoe, 1966

Gaslight Gang, 1969

Razing of old Robinson Gymnasium, 1967

Let me begin with the University of Kansas—in our Centennial year perhaps such lack of modesty might be forgiven—one of the nation's major universities. In undergraduate education it is one of the best, in professional education, one of the better, and in graduate education, one of the good. And in all of these areas, it is constantly improving.

The University of Kansas, in its one hundredth year, has the promise of becoming one of the nation's great universities—and within the decade. The level of its achievements, and the resulting benefits to the entire state and region, are limited only by the dedication of its citizens, the loyalty of its alumni, and the generosity of its friends.

Chancellor W. Clarke Wescoe, "The Second Century," March 1966

New Fraser, 1967

Dancing at the Red Dog Inn, 1967

Greek Week tug-of-war, 1966

Chancellor Wescoe in Topeka, 1968

Spencer Research Library

Twenty-eighth annual cross-country meet at KU, 1966

Dwight Peck and Jim Ryun, 1967

New Haworth Hall, 1968

"Human be-in" at Potter Lake, 1967   Spring, 1967

The sixties scene

I have often talked from this place before
And the platform always stayed beneath my feet
    before
But tonight am I
Sev'ral stories high
When I think of the hill where we've lived.

Here was Lilac Lane in the heart of town
You could hear this Clarke in ev'ry single part of
    town
Here excitement poured
We were never bored
Here on this, on the hill which we love.

But oh, the saddening feeling
Just to know tonight is the last
That new and saddening feeling
That all our fun together quickly will be past.

People stop and stare. They say Chancellor
That's a title I won't have for many moments more
All my time's gone by
I don't care cause I
Lived with you on this hill which we love.

Chancellor W. Clarke Wescoe, Baccalaureate Exercises, June 2, 1969

ROTC demonstration, 1969

CHAPTER SEVEN

Protest and Renewal

IN THIS VOLUME, the time of militant confrontation and dissent against the war in Vietnam passes rather quickly. The half-dozen photographs of protest, of marching, of the burning of the Student Union soon give way to a picture of Chancellor Chalmers in intense, earnest discussion with students about the values of Western Civilization. Then the sequence moves on to the Space Technology Center, to be named after Raymond Nichols, twelfth chancellor, who more than anyone reconciled the University's past with its future. The sculpture in front of that building is of the fallen Icarus, the youth who, in an excess of confidence in his own great skill, flew too close to the sun and so fell back to earth. The initial photographs are very much "news" shots. As such, they might have been taken on any of scores of American campuses. They were not: they were taken on the Hill. Between the PEACE NOW banner and the American flag rises the World War II Memorial Campanile; the Campanile also looms before the burning roof of the World War I Memorial Union. Full-hearted support of those two wars had earlier disrupted campus life; outrage against the one in Southeast Asia "virtually closed down" the University. Indeed, in Memorial Stadium, students voted *en masse* to do just that. The University did not exactly return to normal; no institution does. It did, however, get on with activities more specifically the province of higher education. As the war wound down,

students voted to honor outstanding progressive educators in the same stadium, using the acronym HOPE for the award. A research campus developed to the west, near the burial site of Civil War casualties. Here, Professor Higuchi directed pharmaceutical research; in Moore Hall, the Geological Survey monitored Kansas' petroleum and ground-water reserves; in Nichols Hall, data from space satellites were analyzed and applied to the problems of earth. Many faculty came down off the Hill to teach in the legislative halls of the Capitol, in suburban classrooms in Johnson County, or in a music room at Iola High School. On the Hill, students pondered the problems of social welfare, watched the magic of chemistry, listened to lectures on literature and philosophy in the spacious auditorium of the new School of Religion. The cell-like rooms of the giant dormitories on the Daisy Field Hill could become more personal with memorabilia of the Beatles and Flower Children. Professor Sam Anderson could now arrange his Russian books and artifacts in his first decent office in forty years. Outside of the new Humanities Building students sunned themselves on what was becoming known as "Wescoe beach." High-topped laced boots of the turn-of-the-century, ubiquitous bobby-sox and saddle oxfords of the forties and fifties, the bare feet or sandals of the sixties, all gave way to the jogging shoe.

The final aerial photograph in this volume was made in 1979. The angle of the camera and

197

the addition of so many flat-topped buildings work to obscure the contours of the Hill. The picture fools the eye, and it also calls into question whether "The Hill" is an interchangeable term for "The University." So much of what the University does is not included and could not be comprehended in any picture. Beyond the left frame two large professional schools—Engineering and Law—have moved westward toward the research campus. Law took along the name but not the statue of Uncle Jimmy Green. Old Green has taken the name of a long-neglected chancellor, Lippincott, and become the Center of International Programs, whose activities even a camera placed in a satellite could not register. Nor does the camera here record the largest and most complex of the professional schools, that of Health Sciences. Nevertheless, the aerial photo tells us something about the history of the University. The original topography of the Hill continues to dictate a network of curving roads and walkways. The Groves of Marvin and Potter's pond resist incursion. Spencer Research Library guards the promontory between. The Military Science

building occupies a good bit of ground now coveted as a future site for a science and music library. Above that site, Visual Arts have finally found the well-lighted space they have needed since 1866. Diagonally across is the Museum of Art that Mrs. Spencer gave to house a rapidly growing collection, to mount exhibitions, and, in Franklin Murphy's phrase, to "entrap the unwary student" and provoke curiosity about the currents of human culture. Inside the museum a warmly dressed student contemplates Gerôme's *Two Arabs by a Fireplace* (1882), bought by funds donated by hundreds of alumni, faculty, and other friends of art.

One photograph, apparently taken from atop a Daisy Field dorm, creates a montage of the central campus. Much as has this book, the telescopic lens has arranged the Hill into a series of two-dimensional planes that blend the old with the new. The earliest historic people to stand on the Hill were the Kanza, "People of the South Wind." It is early spring. A stiff but warm southern breeze bends the pines in front of Flint Hall and holds the flags on Fraser.

Vietnam protest, 1970

There have always been people who objected to every war this country fought, but the war in Vietnam is perceived by our students as politically unjustifiable and morally indefensible, and I agree with them on both counts.

Chancellor Laurence Chalmers, speech to the River Club in Kansas City, September 25, 1969

As a private citizen, as a state senator, as a taxpayer, I'm sick and tired of providing a sanctuary for violence, for turmoil, and for disruption at the University of Kansas. I'm sick of the activities of the new left.

Reynolds Schultz, Lawrence, quoted in the *Jayhawker,* 1970.

The first and foremost function of the university is the education of its students. The curriculum and faculty must be oriented toward the cutting edge of society. New left politics are an important effort to check persistent archaic traditions and keep us alert. . . . Student dissent is a healthy sign certainly in contrast to the decade of the fifties where the concern was frequently the apathy of the students.

Chancellor Laurence Chalmers, quoted in the *Jayhawker,* 1970

In 1969, any student who wanted to translate theory into action could find outlets. Some outlets took organized, structured form and were viewed as the flowering of free expression. Other outlets forsook form or rule and were viewed as noxious weeds, free expression gone awry. But outlets abounded, and they gave us choices. I went with structure. . . . I marched—down Jayhawk Boulevard, around the Topeka

Kansas Memorial Union fire, 1970

199

Capitol, down Pennsylvania Avenue in Washington, D.C. That first step off the sidewalk sidelines and into the street was exhilarating. It also was a symbolic cutting loose, for I left friends and roommates walking the other way.

There were dead-of-night trips to Cleveland for rally planning meetings. On those trips, carloads of "doves" sang "Abbey Road" and "Bridge Over Troubled Water," and reassured each other that if Professor Bass flunked them for missing the anthropology test, it was worth it. . . . If any single image of 1969 persists, it is that of confrontation. . . . Most confrontations were the small, private, daily ones, and they left a more lasting legacy. It was almost impossible, in 1969, to get through a day without being confronted by a leaflet, a literature table in one's path, the chance to applaud or harass a speaker, a rally or a march. . . . KU in 1969 had a vibrant atmosphere. Students pursued pure academics, but they also engaged in discourse, if not movement, that had a direct bearing on what was going on

200   Kansas Memorial Union fire, 1970

outside the campus walls. . . .
Explanations . . . are fairly simple. We looked outward in 1969
because we were afraid.

Lynn Anderson, "The Confrontation,"
Kansas Alumni, 1979

The Union had been burned,
people had been killed, the University virtually closed down.
Many were scared, perhaps because they had seen that it was
very easy to burn a building, to
destroy the school's relationship
with the taxpayers, or even to
kill someone. It was another
matter altogether to rebuild what
had been destroyed. By August
of 1970, things had bottomed out
and, in some ways, the history of
KU and Lawrence in the '70s is
that of an institution and a
community on the rebound.

By 1974, when I received my
undergraduate degree, the picture had changed drastically. The
infamous Rock Chalk and Gaslight bars were gone, the penny
papers weren't distributed anymore, the Legislature supported
the University again, and the
broad, green lawns on Mount
Oread were well-tended. Stability
was in the air, or at least the
budget.

Steve Warren, ". . . Damn, it's been
interesting," *Kansas Alumni,* December 1979

While it is true that I am
responsible for everything that
occurs on the campus, my authority is widely delegated and
highly decentralized. Holding the
title of chancellor offers the opportunity to develop consensus
among faculty members, among
staff members, and among students but it does not grant the
right to make unilateral direc-
tives. To attempt to lead a great
university without consensus is as
foolish as it is futile.

Chancellor Laurence Chalmers, quoted in
the *Kansas City Star,* February 21, 1971

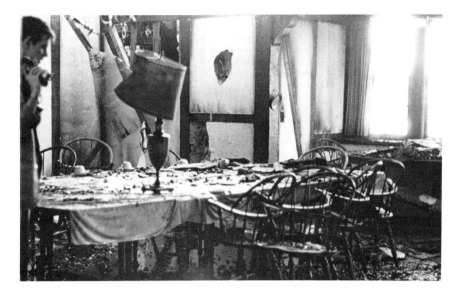

Chancellor Laurence Chalmers with
Western Civilization class, 1970

Nichols Hall, dedicated in 1971

February Sisters protest in 1971

202

HOPE Award winners, 1972 *From far right:* Arno F. Knapper, associate professor of business; Elizabeth Schultz, associate professor of English; John B. Bremner, professor of journalism

Pearson College   Dennis Quinn, professor of English, is at the far left

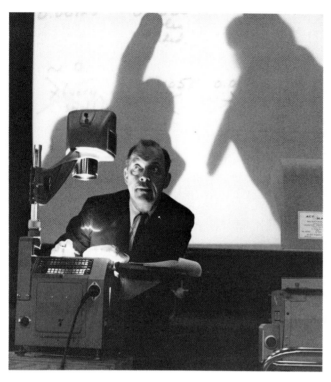

Clark Bricker, professor of chemistry

Student Susan Lominska presents petition to Vice Chancellor
William Balfour, 1973

University administrators, 1973 *Left to right:* Archie Dykes, chancellor; Del Shankel,
associate dean of the College of Liberal Arts and Sciences; Ray Nichols, chancellor emeritus

Contrast in architecture may be somewhat violent in this campus group but the fact is provocative of interest at first sight, however much one may feel the absence of a harmonious effect.

Graduate Magazine, 1915

Lavenia Cooper assists a visitor

Wescoe Hall, dedicated in 1974

Social Welfare class, 1973

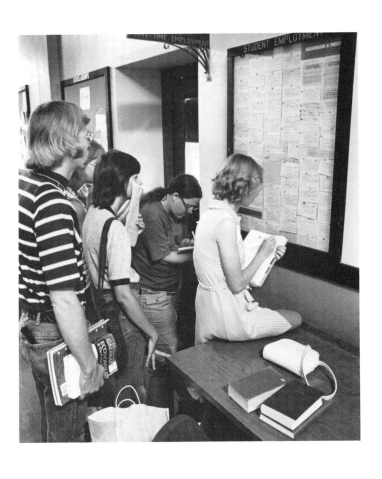

Sledding on the Hill

Streaking on the Hill

Outreach program   Marvin Harder, professor of political science and director of the Capitol Complex, lectures in the state legislative chambers

Howard Boyajian, professor of music performance, meets with high school students in Pittsburg, Kansas

One of the many significant commitments that Kansas University has made under the chancellorship of Archie Dykes is for greater outreach, meaning that increasing thousands of people not only in Kansas but throughout the region will be served by the university. . . . During the past year, more than 60,000 persons were enrolled in one or more programs of KU's Division of Continuing Education, a unit of the outreach effort. These are people who in at least a small way became KU-oriented even though they did not necessarily come to Lawrence or the campus for their courses. The goal of outreach . . . is to offer all KU's teaching resources to the service of as many Kansans as possible, increasing an important two-way involvement. There was a time, in the not-too-distant-past, when KU had an aura of exclusivity about it. Rightly or wrongly, too many regarded the school as something of a closed corporation that had its own views and goals with not a great deal of concern for the so-called outside world. Efforts in recent years, most notably the Outreach and Easy Access programs stimulated by the Dykes regime, have changed that a great deal—and are due to change it even more in the future.

Lawrence Journal-World, July 21, 1975

Dean George R. Waggoner

Takeru Higuchi, Regents Distinguished Professor of Chemistry and Pharmacy

Sam Anderson, associate professor of Soviet and East European studies

Black History Month

Affirmative Action Office   *Left to right:* Robert Cobb, dean of the College of Liberal Arts and Sciences, meets with Mike Edwards, acting director of Affirmative Action

Spencer Museum of Art, dedicated in 1977

At the Spencer Museum dedication *Left to right:* Former chancellors Clark Wescoe, Franklin Murphy, Ray Nichols, and Chancellor Archie Dykes

The dedication of the Helen Foresman Spencer Museum of Art is the culmination . . . of a dream held by some of us for many years. . . . This occasion epitomizes still another example of the enormous, almost disproportionate role that private giving has played in the life and the growth of this great University. . . . We here, today, dedicate a university art museum that for beauty and utility cannot be surpassed anywhere in the country. . . . The objects of art in a university museum are there to be used as tools for teaching, to flesh out and give reality to the words of the lecturer. In a less formal way, . . . this museum and its works of art will surely entrap the unwary student with time on his hands, stimulating first curiosity and then appreciation. One might call this learning by revelation rather than indoctrination. The University museum has an unusual opportunity, and I might add an obligation, to mount exhibitions relating to the teaching programs of many different departments of the University, again permitting the object to illuminate cultural and political history around the globe and across millenia of time.

Franklin Murphy, at the dedication of the
Spencer Art Museum, 1977

Green Hall, dedicated in 1977

Art and Design building, dedicated in 1977

Academic Computer Center, dedicated in 1978

Lynette Woodard

1979

216

The 1926 Men's Glee Club alumni sing at All-University Supper in 1981

Acting Chancellor Del Shankel on a rainy Commencement Day, 1981

Carillon bells restored with funds from Campaign Kansas

CHAPTER EIGHT

Expansion and Preservation

FORTY-FIVE PHOTOGRAPHS to capture, represent, or at least suggest the 1980s at KU. Surely not enough to record what also was the decade of the personal video-camera. That instrument—in the hands of thousands of friends, relatives, coaches, teachers, students, traffic cops—produced thirty frames a second to catch the activities on The Hill. Here, a single shot of Danny Manning in mid-leap; in the archives of the Athletic Department, millions of frames of Manning completing the leap, running, shooting, clapping hands to encourage team-mates, grimacing, smiling. Here, the crowd is an indistinct, mottled-gray background; on the videos, the spectators are animated blue sprinkled with red and white—and they make noise. Coaches in conservative business suits and ties pace and signal and yell. Here, a handful of "still" photos. And they do just that: they "still" or stop or hold for a fraction of a second a moment now devoid of motion, color, sound, a sense of time passing. Or so we often think.

The opening photo of the newly restored carillon is certainly static: the rigid geometry of the framing, the solid bell, the clapper poised to strike the quarter hour or a note commanded by a carillonneur. But almost unaware, viewers of this photo will animate it and place it, so to speak, within their own ongoing videos. Many will hear what—along with the steam whistle and the Rock-Chalk chant—is one of the distinctive sounds of KU. Many will place it in time by remembering that the carillon is housed in the

World War II memorial campanile and that the bells wore themselves out sounding throughout forty years of the Cold War that ended with the decade.

The restored bells sound a significant note of the 1980s: preserved and restored older buildings and generally harmonious new ones. A "sea-change in attitudes," as Dennis Farney said in *Alumni Magazine*, marked the eighties. Instead of buildings razed, there were buildings "recycled," a key word of the time. KU gained modern, useful space while the campus preserved its heritage with extensive renovation of Watson Library, Marvin, Snow, and the Memorial Union. When fire largely destroyed Hoch, the state came up with the money for a renewed Hoch behind the still intact and familiar arched entry. When time ate away at the unusual red sandstone of Spooner, a vigilant Historic Mount Oread Fund successfully encouraged restoration.

New buildings take cues from their historic contexts. The smooth Kansas limestone walls and the pitched red roof of Anschutz Science Library blend with the Collegiate Gothic of its sister library, Watson, and its neighbors, Snow and Hoch. Amini Hall does the same with the Georgian forms of the older scholarship halls. The University Press building brings to West Campus its first rough limestone and pitched red roof of the older campus. The Dole Human Development Center, with its light brick and stepped-back facade, seems the most "Post-Modern," an architectural style of the time that openly refers to the past. Here, the building's round arches echo those of its immediate neighbor to the east and the oldest of surviving KU structures, the Romanesque arcade of KU's original Power Plant. A bit farther east, in the extreme right-hand corner of the photo, is the hillside "Prairie Acre." The university is now restoring this plot to its natural grasslands state. The photograph of the new Lied Center is reminiscent of century-old pictures of North College or Old Fraser; like them, it appears isolated on a prairie knoll. It is not: it anchors the performing arts within the expanding research campus to its south and west and the large Daisy Hill dormitories to the east. KU traditions and future needs shaped these new structures. They continue another KU tradition as well: one, the University Press building, was funded from self-generated sources; one, Dole Center, by the federal government; three major ones—Anschutz, Amini, and Lied—by generous private donors.

Except for the statues in the revived Wilcox Classical Museum and the Chinese boxer guarding the Law School, human figures do not pose formally in this decade. The customary "yearbook" photo of a team, a club, a living group is, for the first time in this book, absent. Marian Washington's Lady Jayhawks and KU Crew are in action; teachers and guest lecturers gesture; the band and supporters of Martin Luther King Day march. Advisors to the Greater University Fund deservedly relax after a highly successful Campaign Kansas drive. Chancellor Budig listens intently to faculty representatives or, with Senator Dole, dons a hardhat. A poet reads; a painter displays his "wears," which reflect faithfully the informal, even "grunge" attire of many students and, alas, faculty as well.

The informality of both photographic technique and human posture and attire may partially mask the intellectual and moral seriousness and intensity of university life. The most informal photographs record engineering students mesmerized by their own ingenuity, future teachers learning sign language, students speaking out against sexual harassment, a young woman monitoring our fragile natural environment. Higuchi awards encourage and support faculty research. Students in shorts and athletic sneakers, the footwear of choice for the second decade in a row, receive the torch of tradition.

The pattern these photographs suggest is an optimistic one. Students and faculty are more diverse than in previous decades; they look "more like America," in the phrase of the newly elected American president. And they are engaged in the intellectual, social, political, and economic issues that engage the nation and the world. Financial support from alumni and friends of KU has been generous. Old and new, past and future, heritage and change, seem to have united more easily in these years than in the eras of world wars, depression, the social and political disruption of the sixties. The Kansas Union, which began as a memorial to the First Great War, has been in a state of almost continuous renovation ever since. A slogan announced its most recent enlargement and remodeling: "Toward a More Perfect Union." Just a catchy, recycled phrase? or a compelling ideal?

Kansas Governor John Carlin congratulates Chancellor Gene Budig at his inauguration, 1981

The University of Kansas is the creation of the people of Kansas. For 116 years they have reaffirmed their conviction that the basis of a democratic society is an educated people. To achieve that end, they have fostered a great university here. I believe the University is ready now to assume an even greater position of leadership in higher education. I intend that we shall do so.

The strengths of this University are many, and they are easy to identify. Our undergraduate, graduate, and professional degree programs are innovative and comprehensive. They are respected as excellent preparation for further study or for a career, and they are respected even more as genuine educational experiences: courses and programs of study which help our students become truly educated young men and women. Students from this University are sought after by business and the professions, and are welcomed into graduate and professional schools across America—for our colleagues know what we too often take for granted: that KU offers each of its students the opportunity for an outstanding education. It is up to our students then to take advantage of what we offer.

Installation address of Gene A. Budig, Chancellor, August 24, 1981

Architecture students congregate in the hallway of Marvin Hall, renovated in 1980 and honored by the Kansas Society of Architects for its lively interior and space utilization

I think there's been a sea change in attitudes. . . . In the '60s a lot of things were torn down nationally and at KU. Now I think there is a new appreciation that some things are worth the effort, and even the cost, to preserve. Because you're preserving more than the structure; you're preserving a heritage.

Dennis Farney, *Kansas Alumni Magazine,* September 1990

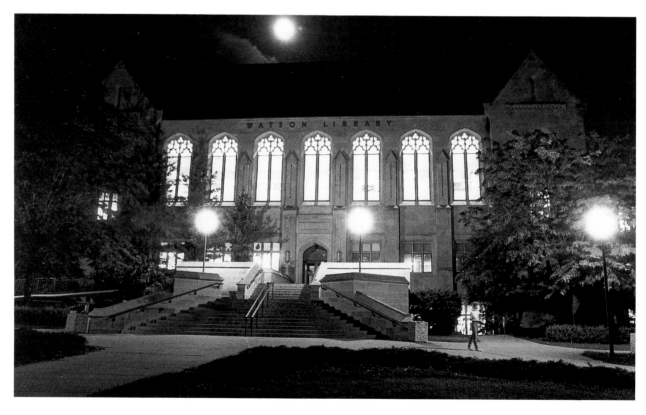

Watson Library, renovated in the early 1980s

Higuchi Award winners, 1982
Left to right: Ralph N. Adams, University Distinguished Professor of Chemistry; Norge W. Jerome, professor of community health and director of the Division of Community Nutrition at the KU Medical Center; John S. Brushwood, Roy A. Roberts Distinguished Professor of Spanish and Portuguese; and Richard L. Schowen, Summerfield Distinguished Professor of Chemistry

Grant Goodman and James Seaver, professors of history, meet with Chancellor Gene Budig, 1982

Dyche Hall is the signature structure at Kansas. It is encrusted with Old World architectural elements like an arcaded loggia, multisided bays, balconies, gables and gablets, projecting and pinnacled pavilions, and a plethora of round arches (except for the modillion-blocked gable over the entrance, modeled after St. Trophime Church in Arles, France). And the tower, which can be seen from half the state, is a character piece of rusticated Oread limestone that soars past double rounded windows, steep gables, cornices, lunettes, and columns; then it is crowned with a steep multisided cone.

But look again. Dyche Hall's exterior is also ornamented with sculptured animal icons both real and mythical—the cowlike heads on the columns. This announces that inside resides one of campusdom's four best natural history museums.

Thomas A. Gaines, *The Campus as a Work of Art*, 1991

I first visited K.U. in the Spring of 1965. On numerous occasions subsequently I have returned to Mount Oread always with happiness to be on such an attractive campus, and with a profound sense of gratitude for Kansan generosity and friendliness.

The high point of my academic career I consider to be the Fall Semester of 1989, which I spent as Rose Morgan Visiting Professor at K.U. I realized, for perhaps the first time, the full meaning of the phrase "a university is a community of scholars." Where else but at K.U. could I, a microbiologist with genetical interests, have interacted not only with like-minded scientists, but also with the German Club, a Professor of Film Studies, the Chairman of the African Studies Dept., and a Professor of Classics, with interests in both ancient and modern Olympic Games? And, too, have attended lectures and seminars on topics as varied as Armenia, AIDS, feminist Norway, plus (American style) football games, basketball games of both sexes of Jayhawks, indoor and outdoor track-and-field meets, plus concerts, films, and exhibitions in the Natural History, Spencer Art, and Anthropology museums. Here is one Limey who is eternally grateful!

Professor Colin Clarke, East Anglia University, Great Britain, 1992

Dyche Museum of Natural History, 1983

Michael Ott, professor of art, Kansas Governor's Artist, 1986

224

Tai Chi Figure, 1985, a sculpture by Ju Ming in front of Green Hall, gift of Dr. and Mrs. W. Clarke Wescoe

Rock Chalk rehearsal in Hoch Auditorium, 1986   Proceeds from the popular revues are donated to the United Way of Douglas County

Hoch Auditorium, 1990

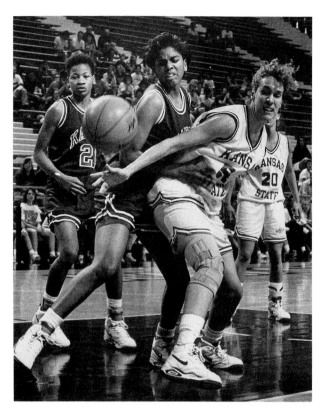

Coach Marian Washington's Lady Jayhawks have played in
three NCAA tournaments since 1980

Coaches Ed Manning and Larry Brown, courtside, 1985

Danny Manning, NCAA Player of the Year, 1988

Pep rally celebrating NCAA basketball championship, 1988

Jubilant Jayhawk basketball team members and supporting staff took turns displaying the 1988 NCAA basketball championship trophy at the pep rally Tuesday afternoon in Memorial Stadium. The event was planned to welcome the team back to Lawrence after its victory over the University of Oklahoma Sooners in the championship game of the NCAA tournament Monday night in Kemper Arena, Kansas City, Mo. The rally, which attracted about 30,000 wildly cheering fans, followed a night of celebrating on campus. Classes were canceled Tuesday. The Jayhawk team has been invited to Washington Monday, April 11, to meet government leaders. Wednesday, April 13, the Jayhawks will be honored with a 4 p.m. parade in downtown Lawrence.

Oread, April 8, 1988

Martin Luther King Day parade, Jayhawk Boulevard, 1988

Wilcox Classical Museum exhibit in Lippincott Hall, opened in 1988, a century after the original installation in Old Fraser Hall

In 1888 the Classical Museum of the University of Kansas Department of Ancient Languages and Literatures was dedicated at the June Commencement. The plaster casts then placed on exhibition on the second floor of Old Fraser Hall in the quarters of what was to become the Department of Classics formed the nucleus of a collection which grew in the years following largely through the efforts of A. M. Wilcox, Professor of Greek from 1865 to 1915; the Collection is named in his honor. It was Professor Wilcox's aim to put Kansans in touch with the great traditions of the Greeks and Romans in the visual arts in an era when travel to the museums of Europe was a luxury for the wealthy, the quality of photographs and slides was poor, and original works of ancient art were not yet available in the area. . . . After Old Fraser Hall was closed in 1965, the Wilcox casts suffered considerable damage during 20 years of storage in various locations on and off campus. . . . The Gallery is named for Mary Amelia Grant, Emerita Associate Professor of Classics, longtime Curator and benefactress of the Collection.

Mary Amelia Grant Gallery, Wilcox Classical Museum brochure

Campaign Kansas has changed the University of Kansas forever. When we began planning this historic effort eight years ago, we hoped it would have a positive influence on KU faculty, students and academic programs. . . . The $260 million for students, museum and library materials, research and faculty support will significantly enhance the excellent education offered at the University of Kansas. We are extremely grateful to the thousands of KU friends who have made this fund drive so successful.

Jordan L. Haines, *Campaign Kansas Action Report,* Summer 1992

The *New York Times Selective Guide to Colleges* rates America's finest universities and assigns one to five stars to each school, representing each institution's academic strength. The University of Kansas, with four stars, ranks higher than any other Big Eight school. "Fifth Star Rising" is the theme of the CAMPAIGN KANSAS celebration May 12, 1988.

Campaign Kansas brochure, 1988

Robert Riss, national vice chairman of Campaign Kansas, kicks off fund drive, 1988

Greater University Fund advisory board at Adams Alumni Center, 1989
The center was dedicated in 1983, the alumni association's centennial year

The Marian and Fred Anschutz Science Library, dedicated in 1989

Vice Chancellor Frances Horowitz, Chancellor Gene Budig, and Senator Bob Dole inspect the Dole Human Development Center construction site, 1989

Dole Human Development Center, 1990

"Goldberg Gus," winner of 1990 Rube Goldberg competition, was designed by six mechanical engineering students

KU cheerleaders, yell leaders, and Baby Jay, 1989

1989/90 KU crew

Alice-Ann Darrow, professor of music education, teaches American sign language

Richard Stevens, KU senior, checks course lists at
Strong Hall enrollment center, 1992

Kansas Senator Wint Winter addresses student senate orientation, 1990

Blake Hall and Twente Hall above the Wakarusa Valley, 1990

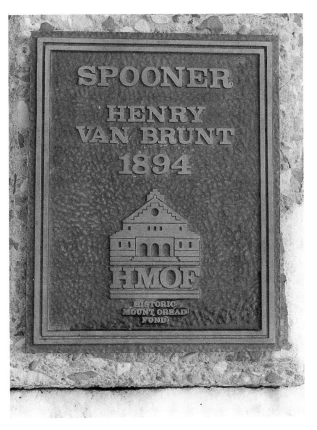

Historic Mount Oread Fund bronze marker placed near Spooner, 1990

The Historic Mount Oread Fund has presented bronze plaques to be placed on the 10
oldest buildings on KU's Lawrence campus. . . . The plaques will be placed on
Spooner, Stauffer-Flint, Dyche, Marvin,
Lippincott, Bailey, Strong and Snow halls,
Hoch Auditorium and Watson Library. . . .
The historic fund, founded in 1981, is
devoted to the preservation of buildings,
sites and amenities on the Lawrence campus.

Oread, April 13, 1990

Dedication of Old North College Historic Site, April, 1991   In front of the Mortar Board Fire Basket are Chancellor Budig (left) and Dennis Farney, president of the Historic Mount Oread Fund

The landscaped plot adjacent to Gertrude Sellards Pearson and Corbin halls on the Lawrence campus commemorates the site of Old North College. Brass plaques mark several artifacts:

North College Threshold   Footsteps of students and faculty who passed through the building during its 53 years have grooved the stone. Lillian Ross Leis, one of KU's first students, wrote that the North College steps made "a most pleasant place to linger."

North College Stone Window Sill   This stone window sill, mounted here on a pedestal, was preserved by the W. R. Green family.

Fire Basket   This cast-iron fire basket was a gift to the university in 1927 from the Torch Chapter of Mortar Board, an honor society for seniors. In freshman induction ceremonies from 1924 to the 1960s, upperclassmen would pass to new students a torch lit by a bonfire in the basket. The ritual symbolized the passing of knowledge. A version of the torch passing ritual survives today during Traditions Night, a fall semester ceremony for entering freshmen.

Old North College 1866 Historic Site, pamphlet published by the KU Office of University Relations, April 1991

Ken Irby, KU poet, participates in *Moby-Dick* Marathon
reading on the centennial of Melville's death, 1991

KU Traditions Night, 1991

The destruction of Hoch Auditorium brought back many memories, beginning with my return to KU as chancellor in 1939. My inauguration was held in Hoch at the Opening Convocation, and I remember marching down the aisle in full academic regalia, behind the members of the Board of Regents. Feeling a tug at my gown, I glanced around to see my old Harvard roommate, Santry Reed, a KU Phi Gam who had come for the occasion from his home in Newton. The occasion seemed to go off well and at the conclusion there was a luncheon for the chief dignitaries in the English Room of the Student Union. My father was there, but I think I failed to invite Charles Moreau Harger of Abilene, who was chairman of the Board of Regents.

I remember hearing operatic soloist Grace Moore in Hoch. She was later killed when her plane was shot down by enemy fire along the west coast of France during World War II. Miss Moore's concert was so crowded that we had students on the stage. About every fifth number, Miss Moore would simply turn her back on the vast audience of at least 3,500 and sing to the people on the stage—a gracious act of thoughtfulness.

A renowned speaker at Hoch was Otto of Austria, the attractive young crown prince and heir to the throne of the Austro-Hungarian Empire. After his family was thrown out, he took to the lecture circuit, not defending his position but giving some admirable lectures on current affairs.

Hoch was also the scene of a memorial service following Chancellor Ernest Lindley's death at sea in 1939 on his return from a year's leave of absence. Mrs. Lindley was afraid the auditorium would look funereal, but my wife, Eleanor, masterful as always, arranged for two huge jardinieres of autumn leaves that with the dark red curtains behind made a lovely, non-funereal background. Mrs. Lindley was most effusive in her appreciation.

Hoch will live in the memories of thousands of students and faculty. It was a beautiful building, happily used for so many events, and will long live in the hearts of loyal Jayhawkers.

Deane W. Malott, *Kansas Alumni Magazine,* November/December 1991

Hoch Auditorium burns after it was struck by lightning June 15, 1991

University Press of Kansas building on West Campus, dedicated 1991

Completed in 1991, our new home at 2501 West 15th Street has enabled the University Press of Kansas to continue to expand into the 1990s. Over the last decade the press has quadrupled the number of scholarly titles that it publishes in a year, and we now sell annually more than 100,000 books throughout the world. Our growth has strengthened our ability to extend the reach and reputation of the six state universities that sponsor our operation.

Fred M. Woodward, director, University Press of Kansas

Students learn film lighting techniques in Oldfather Studio, 1992

Lied Center for the Performing Arts under construction on West Campus, 1992

Max Falkenstien interviews Tony Sands and football coach Glen Mason
after Sands set NCAA single-game rushing record in Missouri game, 1991

Head basketball coach Roy Williams and assistants Mark Turgeon
and Steve Robinson

Sylvia Stone of the Women's Studies staff reads testimonials at the sexual
harassment speak-out in 1992

Kristen Bradel, environmental studies student,
sampling prairie vole populations at the Kansas
Ecological Reserve, 1992

Amini Scholarship Hall, gift of K. K. Amini, 1992

Scholarship halls provide the best environment for students. By living at Battenfeld Hall, I made a lot of friends. . . . I got a chance when I really needed it, and now I'd like to make it possible for others to find that same opportunity. . . . Maybe someday one of these young men will be able to reciprocate, continuing this tradition in the University of Kansas.

K. K. Amini, *Campaign Kansas Action Report*, Winter 1991

The Palladian window which now marks the entry to Amini Hall's living room was salvaged from the handsome old house which occupied the Amini site. The window was located directly above the front entry at the central stair landing. During the planning for Amini, the University expressed a strong interest in respecting the character and history of the surrounding residential neighborhood. When it proved infeasible to renovate or relocate the existing house, we looked for a way to incorporate some part of the house within the new scholarship hall. The relocation of the window from the old entry to the new seemed an appropriate gesture, and the arched top of the window signals the inspiration for the arched top windows throughout Amini.

Jackson Clark, project manager for Gould Evans Associates, architect for Amini Hall

Building "a more perfect Union," Kansas Union renovation, 1992

Nearly every class that has attended the University of Kansas since the 1920s will have a different memory of the Kansas Union. Since its placement at its present site in 1924, the building has been under constant change and remodeling.

The first Kansas Union was started in 1914 in a small building at 1200 Tennessee St. The building was closed after one year because the University could not pay the rent. Because the building was so far from campus, students did not go to the Union enough to generate necessary revenue.

After World War I, the administration decided that a student union should be built in memory of an estimated 130 former students who had died serving in the war.

The University raised $210,000 for the project, and the groundbreaking took place at the 1925 Commencement.

The Memorial Union was dedicated in 1927, and in the following years various portions of the building were added, including the Ballroom in 1933, the Old English Room in 1938, and the Kansas Room in 1939.

In 1928 the Union Operating Committee was set up to manage the Memorial Union, and the Student Union Activities Board was set up to coordinate social activities.

A three-year renovation began in 1950, when the University spent $2.25 million to double the size of the old structure, bringing the Union close to its present size.

In 1946 the students decided to rename the Union by dropping "Memorial" from the name because they thought that a memorial only for World War I casualties made little sense in the aftermath of World War II.

In the late 1960s another addition was completed at a cost of more than $1 million. But soon after the completion, tragedy struck.

In April 1970, fire ravaged the Union. The cause of the fire was considered arson, and during the turbulent times of the unpopular Vietnam War and massive student unrest, the National Guard was called in, and a curfew was imposed on students.

The Union's main structure survived the fire, and in 1971 remodeling was completed. Throughout the next 20 years the Union went through other large-scale renovations and additions, culminating in the work that is in progress.

The new renovations will give the front of the Union a new look with large plate glass windows and a terrace on the South side of the third floor.

Overall the additions will cost close to $10 million, but as the students of KU have seen over the past 70 years the additions probably will not be the last.

The University Daily Kansan, August 19, 1992

Band centennial 1992—"Jayhawks marching into the next century"

Waving the wheat

Photography Credits

All photographs are from the University Archives, Spencer Research Library, except those listed below, which are used courtesy of the following individuals and organizations.

Rebecca Bauman, for University Relations: left p. 235
Daron J. Bennett, for the *University Daily Kansan:* bottom left p. 238
Jonathan Blumb: top p. 214, bottom p. 214; for the Spencer Art Museum, top p. 225
R. Benecke, from DeGolyer Library, Southern Methodist University: bottom p. 28
Ben Bigler, for the *Lawrence Journal-World:* top left p. 231
Ron Bishop: top p. 200
Bob Blank, for the *Jayhawker:* top right p. 155
Kip Chin, for the *University Daily Kansan:* bottom left p. 232
Rich Clarkson: bottom p. 158, top left p. 193
Duke D'Ambra: lower p. 94, top p. 95, bottom p. 98, bottom left p. 99, top p. 102, bottom p. 102, bottom p. 104, top p. 108, bottom p. 108, top p. 109, bottom p. 110, top p. 111, p. 112, bottom p. 114, p. 115, top p. 116, top p. 117, bottom p. 118, p. 119, p. 123, p. 125, top p. 131, top p. 137, bottom p. 138, bottom p. 139, top p. 140, top p. 141, bottom p. 141, bottom p. 143, top p. 145, bottom p. 146, bottom p. 147, bottom p. 148, bottom p. 149, bottom p. 150, p. 151, bottom left p. 155, top p. 156, bottom p. 157, top p. 158, top p. 159, bottom p. 160, bottom right p. 165, top p. 169, top p. 170, top p. 171, top p. 172, bottom p. 174, top p. 176, bottom p. 177, bottom p. 178, top left p. 179, top p. 184, bottom p. 185
Diane Debinski: bottom right p. 238
Jerry DeNoyelles: bottom right p. 238
Steve Dick, for University Relations: p. 227, top p. 228, top p. 237
Wally Emerson, for the Endowment Association, p. 218
Homer Frank: bottom p. 206
Alexander Gardner, from Kansas State Historical Society, Topeka: p. 12; from Missouri Historical Society, St. Louis: top p. 14
Graduate Magazine: top p. 132, bottom p. 133
Jayhawker: p. 199, top p. 213, top p. 215, bottom p. 215, bottom p. 216, bottom p. 217
Jennifer Jewett, for University Relations: top right, bottom left, p. 230
Jeff Johnston, for University Relations: bottom right p. 230, right p. 235
Doug Koch, for the Endowment Association: right p. 229
Lawrence Journal-World: top left p. 190, bottom p. 202, both p. 208
Jack Long, for the Alumni Association: bottom p. 159
Joseph L. Lies, for University Relations: top right p. 231
David McKinney, for University Relations: p. 234, p. 236

Holly McQueen: p. 241
JoAnn Marinelli: p. 198
Gary Mason: p. 196
Jan M. Morris, for the *University Daily Kansan:* top p. 232
Shari Oettins, for the *University Daily Kansan:* bottom p. 224
Tim Ontko: top p. 211
Oread: top p. 205, bottom p. 209, top p. 210, bottom p. 210, bottom p. 211, bottom p. 213, top p. 217, top p. 218, bottom p. 218
I. L. Pfalzer: bottom p. 144
Glen A. Phillips, for the Alumni Association: top p. 183, top right p. 194
Dennis Quinn: bottom p. 203
Earl Richardson, for the Endowment Association: p. 239
A. Ronnig, for University Relations: top p. 233
Mary Ann I. Saunders, for the Endowment Association: bottom p. 237
Carol Shankel: top p. 212, bottom p. 228, bottom p. 233, middle p. 237, p. 240
Spencer Art Museum: top left p. 192
Ethan Smith: bottom p. 21
Keith Thorpe, for the *University Daily Kansan:* bottom right p. 232
Jim Tice: top p. 163
Topeka Daily Capital: top right p. 189, bottom left p. 191
Richard F. Treece: p. 73, bottom right p. 99
University Daily Kansan: top p. 130, top p. 144, center p. 201, top p. 203, top right p. 204, top left p. 226
University of Kansas Alumni Association: bottom p. 173, top right p. 190, bottom right p. 191, bottom p. 193
University of Kansas *Alumni Magazine:* bottom p. 169
University of Kansas Athletic Department: top right p. 187
University of Kansas Endowment Association: left p. 229
University of Kansas News Bureau: bottom p. 176
University of Kansas Photographic Bureau: top p. 160
University of Kansas Press: bottom p. 162
University of Kansas Sports Information Office: top left and right p. 238
University of Kansas University Relations: p. 2, bottom p. 222, bottom p. 223, top p. 224
Kent van Hoesen: top p. 206
Stephen Wade, for University Relations: bottom p. 225
Watkins Community Museum: bottom p. 140; courtesy of Jane Stevens: top p. 83
Garrett Whitney, for the Alumni Association: top left p. 194
Oz Wille: top p. 211
Margaret Wulfkuhle: p. 20
Hank Young: bottom p. 201; for the Alumni Association, both p. 217
Ed Zurga, for the *University Daily Kansan:* right p. 226

Index

246